Creating a Life with God

CREATING
a Life
G*with*OD

The Call of Ancient
Prayer Practices

DANIEL WOLPERT

UPPER
ROOM BOOKS®
NASHVILLE

CREATING A LIFE WITH GOD
The Call of Ancient Prayer Practices
Copyright © 2003 Daniel Wolpert
All rights reserved.

The Upper Room® Web site: www.upperroom.org

Unless otherwise noted, Scripture quotations are from the New Revised Standard Version Bible, copyright 1989, Division of Christian Education of the National Council of the Churches of Christ in the United States of America. Used by permission. All rights reserved.

Scripture noted AP is the author's paraphrase.

Cover and interior design: UDG|Designworks
Cover illustration: Kevin Tolman, Artville
First printing: 2003

LIBRARY OF CONGRESS CATALOGING-IN-PUBLICATION DATA
Wolpert, Daniel, 1959—
  Creating a life with God : the call of ancient prayer practices /
Daniel Wolpert.
    p. cm.
  ISBN 0-8358-9855-5
  1. Prayer. I. Title.
  BV220.W65 2003
  248.3'2—dc21   2003003839

Printed in the United States of America

To Debra, Sam, and Max,
who every day teach me about creating
a life with God

CONTENTS

ACKNOWLEDGMENTS

*I*n many ways, I find writing this part of the book the most difficult and humbling. It is like a near-death experience in which my life flashes before my eyes, and I see how truly indebted I am to so many people who have helped me, taught me, put up with me, and even learned from me. I really cannot even begin to name them all.

I begin by thanking God from whom all blessings flow. Living in northwest Minnesota means that one encounters, and kills, a lot of mosquitoes. Yet every time I crush one, I realize that I am destroying a marvel of engineering that, compared to a welding robot, for example, is a thing of beauty and brilliance and is something I could never produce. So without the amazing creativity of the Divine Persons, I never could have begun to write a book about creating a life with God.

Then I must acknowledge all those who have taught me the spiritual craft. I have been blessed by encounters with a number of remarkable spiritual teachers, both before and after being baptized. I think particularly of Father Poulin, who baptized me, and Bede Griffiths, who not only baptized my wife but also taught us so much about contemplative Christianity.

All whom I encountered recently in the programs of Christian spirituality at San Francisco Theological Seminary not only have given me wonderful opportunities to work and pray but also have served as a supportive Christian community for me and my family. Then there are the people of Crookston, Minnesota, and the First Presbyterian Church, who are willing to struggle with us as we together attempt to determine what it means to witness as the church in the world.

Finally I would like to thank Robin Pippin and all those at Upper Room Books, who for some reason believed in me and in this project. I continue to count Robin's support for me, an untested writer, as one of the great miracles of my life.

Peace,
DANIEL WOLPERT
Crookston, Minnesota

FOREWORD

I could barely make out Daniel's words through the pop and crackle of the radio. I held the receiver to my ear: ". . . the demons . . . are in place . . . the abba is ready. . . . We're good to go." I smiled, clipped the walkie-talkie to my belt, and skidded down a large sand dune toward the group. It looked like a hostage situation: sixty high school students and fifteen adults all in white blindfolds. They stood in a single winding line, their ears cocked and attentive, each person placing a hand on the shoulder in front. We walked up and over mounds of sand, the sun bright and warm, brief patches of coastal fog drifting over and among us. At last we came to a secluded place surrounded by rolling sand dunes, native grasses, and clusters of craggy cypress trees. The group sat down and removed their blindfolds.

There in front of us sat an abba, a desert father, dressed in rough and fraying burlap. His face was rugged and bearded. He sat in front of burnt logs and ashes. With closed eyes he rocked back and forth, his hands weaving a small cloth. We all sat in silence, taking in the figure. Then slowly, in the quiet within the breeze we began to hear his words, slow and steady, "Jesus, . . . Son of God, . . . have mercy on me. Jesus, . . . Son of God, . . . have mercy on me."

Suddenly a group of ghostlike figures draped in shimmering fabric began to creep over the dunes, whispering all kinds of distractions to him: "You're wasting your time. . . . You think you're holier than others. . . . You should have gotten married and had a useful career. . . ." Saint Anthony continued to pray, continually calling on the name of Jesus to keep his spirit directed toward God. Slowly the demons retreated. Silence. Then Saint Anthony stood and greeted us. He told his life story and invited questions from the young seekers. He taught the Jesus Prayer and summoned the group to spend the rest of the afternoon praying it in the solitude of the desert wilderness. We wandered out across the dunes, finding places to sit and open ourselves to the presence of God.

This is the image that comes to me when I think of Daniel Wolpert. In 1999, the Youth Ministry and Spirituality Project was leading a weeklong spiritual retreat for a group of high school student leaders. For weeks Daniel had been studying and praying, preparing to play the role of Saint Anthony, one of the desert fathers. Together we were seeking to help these students experience and explore the rich praying tradition within the Christian faith.

I had asked Daniel to play the role of Saint Anthony because I see him as a living desert father. He is one of those rare Christian pilgrims who have foregone career and comforts in order to spend long periods of their lives in prayerful solitude seeking to know and be transformed by the presence of Christ. He has lived in monasteries and intentional Christian communities. He has spent years practicing and teaching spiritual direction. He has led numerous silent and spiritual formation retreats.

Creating a Life with God is the fruit of Daniel's years of searching and struggling to know and receive God. Unlike Daniel, few of us have hitchhiked to Alaska on a spiritual quest, driven a broken-down truck cross-country to pray in a Nova Scotian monastery, or ridden overcrowded buses through India searching for the living Christ. And yet Daniel recognizes that all of us are living the life of the seeker; all of us long to let our desire for God burn within us—refusing to reduce our faith to a "ministry" or career. Daniel knows this hunger, this desire, and he has given us a book that responds to it.

Daniel is a pray-er. He knows the pain, boredom, and joy of silence. He knows the anxiety of waiting for a word from God. He knows what it's like to have your life slowly altered and transformed through regular periods of prayer.

Daniel is also a guide. He has served in local and national settings as pastor, spiritual director, and retreat leader. He has spent hundreds of hours listening to the spiritual longings of teenagers and retirees, ministers and laypeople, seekers and lifelong Christians. *Creating a Life with God* is sensitive to the variety of spiritual longings and resistances that arise in the human heart.

The techniques of prayer, as Daniel states, "are amusingly easy." And yet we seem to need permission. We need space. We need companions. This book offers all of these. We are all like the students I led into the desert, blind and groping, hands grasping the shoulder in front of us, stumbling out toward God. And yet God has given us guides, teachers who point the way. Daniel is one of these teachers.

As you read these pages, know that this is more than a "guidebook." It is an invitation to join Jesus in prayer. It is an invitation to recognize and tend the longing of your heart. As you read these pages, may you deepen your awareness of the God behind the practices, the God who waits between the words.

And as you pray, know that you are not alone—that sometime today, somewhere in the Minnesota plains, Daniel Wolpert is also sitting and praying. He is sitting with the desert mothers and fathers. He is sitting with Benedict and Julian, with Francis and Hildegard, Ignatius and Anthony. He is sitting in prayer, opening to the One who loves us, the One who holds and guides us. He is sitting with you and me.

May this work encourage and lead you into the timeless community of Christian pray-ers who continue to welcome the living Christ into the world.

MARK YACONELLI
Codirector, Youth Ministry and Spirituality Project
San Francisco Theological Seminary

INTRODUCTION

My first awakening to the spiritual life and to the life of prayer occurred when I was twenty years old. I had finished college, and I decided to hitchhike from the Bay Area in California to Alaska. I was on a quest—for what I wasn't too sure. I cared deeply about the world, about the problems of the day, and yet my involvement with politics and other secular approaches to these problems always left me feeling vaguely dissatisfied. They never seemed to quite get at the heart of the matter.

At the time I knew nothing about contemplative prayer. For me prayer meant reading the lines in the church bulletin or speaking a formula at meals. So it was unusual that as I got ready for my trip, I found myself sliding a book on contemplation into my backpack.

Later, as I read this book by the side of the road in the vast wilderness of the Yukon and beyond, I suddenly realized that here was something that reached down into the core of our dilemma as human beings. Here was something that struck a blow at the evil separating us from one another and preventing us from loving our brothers and sisters. That something was this different kind of prayer— a deep conversation with God beginning with communion and leading to transformation.

Today I still feel deeply convicted about the value of contemplative prayer. And it is this passion and vision, first kindled many years ago, that inspires this book. We are creatures who are lost and confused, trapped in the maze of our own little view of the world, and the only way out of that maze is the lifeline God offers us. Yet often we cannot even see that salvation—the solution to our estrangement from the divine—is right under our noses. Prayer opens our eyes. Prayer illuminates our minds, enabling the love of God to permeate all that we do.

This book is truly about life with God: a life in which the awareness and consciousness of God sweep us off our feet the way a lover would. It is about taking on the mind of Christ, a process that is a journey, the journey of prayer. When we sit down and begin to pray, we enter into a new land, a land of many surprises, many challenges, and many rewards. Even though we enter this land immediately as we begin to pray, we must cross it; we have not reached the destination at the outset.

Just as I did, many people start with the understanding that prayer is nothing more than speaking formulas or appealing to God for help. I hope you will begin to encounter something much more rich and profound as you read this book. For my desire is that you read not only to obtain information or to learn a prayer technique but also to pray. At first you might read simply to understand the literal meaning of sentences as with prayers in a church bulletin. But perhaps soon you will find yourself drawn into the process in such a way that you begin to relate to something deeper than words on a page. Through your reading and reflecting, you feel called and compelled to relate directly to God.

This type of deeper prayer doesn't happen right away; it takes time to adjust to this new way of being with God. After I returned from my trip, I began to spend time in silence, trying to undertake this new way of praying. Most of the time, all I got for my efforts was a sore back and numb legs. However, slowly but surely, something began to happen. I began to be aware that I was not alone in my prayer, that this thing called contemplation truly led to an encounter with the living Jesus.

The slow transformation in our experience of praying is the journey, and the vehicles for this journey are the practices described in this book. In addition, each chapter features a historical figure (or figures) associated with the prayer practice. These pray-ers used, created, or have made the disciplines available to us. And we need them, for our journey is both solitary and communal. It is our path and it is the path of the church. The figures in this book are traveling companions. They are people who have walked "the Way" (the original name of Christianity) before us; when we enter into prayer, we who seek Christ today stand on their shoulders, hoping to see the risen Jesus as he goes before us down the dusty roads of this broken world.

Throughout the book I quote from writings by these historical figures and other sources that reveal these ancient journeys to us. The citations are noted in parentheses, simply giving the short title of the book and the page number of the reference. You will find the complete bibliographic listings for these sources in the References section.

THE PRACTICE OF PRAYER

But why "practice" prayer? People often ask this question. They insist that they pray all the time, not just at some specified hour of the day. People resist putting a set time for prayer in their Day-Timer.

As Paul tells us, prayer without ceasing (1 Thess. 5:17) is the goal of the spiritual life, and we will meet one person, the pilgrim (chapter 3), who took this goal very seriously. However, given the reality of our human condition, we delude ourselves if we believe we can be aware of God at every moment without any sort of practice. Such a feat would be comparable to competing in the Olympics without ever training or practicing a sport.

A prayer practice is just that: practice. It is taking time to learn how to listen for God. It is taking time to see the hand of God at work in our lives. We need to take this time because this listening, this seeing are difficult tasks. I once introduced a time of silent prayer at a prayer service by saying, "Let us take some time to listen to God." One woman who was struggling with various concerns said, "I listen and all I hear is the fan on the ceiling." God's voice is often very soft.

Prayer practice is the art of setting aside our own individual desires to seek the desire that God has placed on our heart. It is becoming aware of the distractions of our minds and then letting them go, and as we repeat the disciplines over time, we become more skilled at seeing God in all that we do.

SENSING GOD'S PRESENCE

What does "seeing God" or "hearing God's voice" actually mean? This is an important question. First of all, I am not talking about seeing apparitions or hearing an actual voice in our head (although neither of these possibilities is out of the question). I am referring to any experience that gives us a hint of something "other" than ourselves at work in the universe.

As we shall see in the following chapters, each of these prayer practices gives us the opportunity to experience this sense of "other" in different ways. We can hear God through a feeling, a thought, a picture, an action, a person, total silence. Yet because all these voices may not be "of God," we need to practice discerning God's voice through the repetition of prayer!

God may first appear as a momentary flicker in our consciousness, a shadow that flits almost imperceptibly across the backdrop of our thoughts. Then we may have a thought that we think is "of God," but we are not sure. Slowly, after many hours, days, weeks, even years, we begin to know with greater certainty when we do "hear God's voice" (although if we ever feel absolutely sure, we are probably wrong).

In conjunction with an increased sense of God's presence, our practice begins to bear fruit in our work, our play, our family, and our relationships. We begin to move freely with the Spirit as we notice God moment to moment. The prayer practice is not the goal but the means to the spiritual life. The historical figures you'll read about here created the practices and integrated them into their faith lives with this aim.

In view of that last statement, a word of caution is in order. We may be tempted to believe that these prayer practices were invented at a single point in time, that one certified holy person created each practice and put it into use in the church. This is simply not the case. Every one of the practices in this book has been prayed in some form since people first began to search for God.

People have always used scripture, silence, creativity, symbol, body, and reflection to seek the signs of the divine in their everyday lives. In fact, all of us already use these things, but most of the time we are not conscious of this process of seeking. All a particular form of prayer does is to organize, mark, and make intentional the search for God, which is already under way in each and every one of us. Prayer is nothing more than conversation with a partner whose presence is elusive—God isn't here in material form, so we use all the resources at our disposal to enter into this conversation.

HISTORY AND THE TRAVELING COMPANIONS

Despite the universal nature of prayer practices, at points in the history of our faith, particular people in particular places did lift up certain prayer methods. In these moments the prayer practices took on a clarity that propelled them into the consciousness of the larger church. They became available to a greater audience than before; they became part of the faith's common vocabulary. The people profiled in this book represent a small cross section of those who occupy such pivotal positions in Christian history.

Before I say more about these important pray-ers, let me comment on my use of history. In the past thirty years, postmodernism has changed our understanding of history from a recitation of "objective facts" to a narration of "stories." History no longer can be said to have happened one certain way; rather we pick and choose ways to tell the story of history. Some people even assert that there is no such thing as history; instead we write our own projections onto the blank slate of the past.

This book is not a history book. As I tell a small bit about the people I have chosen to highlight, I am not relating everything about their social and cultural situations. I am not trying to give you a full analysis of these people and their times. I am telling you a story, and this story is a simplification distorted by my own prejudices, views, and desires.

So it is important that I share with you my basic prejudice, which is this: Whatever the particular situation in which these people found themselves (and of course, as premodern people, they were not aware of their circumstances in the same sense we are as we regard them from a distance in time), somehow God spoke powerfully through them. Somehow the Spirit took root in them in their place and their time, and others around them saw this manifestation of the mind of Christ. The brief accounts I tell here attempt to capture this "spiritual essence" of their stories. I realize that their stories may be told in many ways and have facets I do not talk about, but I believe that God spoke through these people. Furthermore, I believe that they heard God's voice at least in part because of the way they prayed; therefore, it is worthwhile for us to know about, share, and learn from these methods of prayer.

Most of these people lived in monastic communities, which is not surprising since these communities have always incubated the practice of prayer. In the past century, these communities dwindled, and in the Christian West, most of them have died out. Yet the practice of prayer has not died with them; rather we have witnessed an explosion of interest in prayer and contemplation among those of us who live our lives in the so-called secular world.

Looking at these parallel changes over time, it is as if the fruits of prayer ripened on the monastic vine, and as the plant has withered, the ripened pods have broken open, scattering the seeds on the face of the earth to bear new fruit in all of creation.

TWELVE PRAYER PRACTICES

The purpose of this book is to help nourish such new growth, and to that end, the chapters present twelve prayer practices along with corresponding historical figures. Each chapter describes how to use the prayer practice either alone or in groups.

For those who lead groups, it is essential to become familiar with the prayer practices by doing each one yourself before teaching it to others. An overview of the material may be helpful. The first two chapters are fundamental to all that follows. Chapter 1 uses the desert mothers and fathers to focus on the general practices of solitude and silence, key elements to any prayer practice because these disciplines cultivate the skill of listening essential to all the practices. The second chapter describes the practice of *lectio divina,* or sacred reading. This prayer practice grounds the seeker in the world of scripture. Sacred reading takes seriously the contention that the Bible is the Word of God; the purpose of the practice is to hear how God speaks here and now through the Word. The traveling companion for this practice will be Saint Benedict.

The next five chapters describe prayer practices that are primarily "mental" in nature. These practices focus on using the mind to come to know God: the Jesus Prayer, silent contemplative prayer, the examen, creativity, and journaling. The corresponding historical figures for these practices are the pilgrim, the unknown author of *The Cloud of Unknowing*, Ignatius of Loyola, Hildegard of Bingen, and Julian of Norwich. All these people used their mental faculties in powerful ways to deepen their prayer lives.

Chapters 8 and 9 shift the focus from our minds to our created bodies. Body prayer (chapter 8) and the labyrinth (chapter 9) are both means by which we can pray with the material being God has given us. Chapter 8 uses a biblical resource, the Song of Solomon, to show how we can relate to our bodies as a house of prayer; and chapter 9 explores the example of the many Christian communities that have used walking as a means of making the journey of prayer visible and real.

The last three chapters take us beyond our individual selves and seek to show how we can incorporate the world and our lives into our prayer life. Nature, our livelihood, and our community are the prayer practices in these final chapters, and these practices are accompanied by Francis of Assisi, the Beguines (a group of women in the late Middle Ages), and, once again, Saint Benedict. With these final prayer practices, it is now possible to pray deeply within any aspect of our existence.

As we meet these figures who come to us from the distant past, as we learn these prayer practices and begin to integrate them into our lives, we gain strength for the journey. We become more intimate with God, and we become more skilled at listening to God's call for us. We meet Jesus along the Way—the way to love, the way to healing, the path of peace.

Allow yourself to be drawn in. Allow yourself to follow Jesus into the mists of your mind. Cry out to God in the depths of your soul and wait for the reply. Pray while you read this book. It is my hope and prayer that all who open these pages will embark upon this sacred journey.

ONE

SOLITUDE AND SILENCE
The Journey Begins

TRAVELING COMPANIONS
Desert Mothers and Fathers

*Why is silence necessary
for listening, and
what happens when
we enter into the
silence of solitary prayer?
We begin to let go of ourselves,
which allows us
to hear God.*

*P*erhaps the following experience sounds familiar to you: You decide to spend some time praying. Maybe you'll stop by the church during the day. Or maybe you have set up a special place in your house with an altar, a picture, or a candle. Perhaps you have a favorite outdoor spot, and you are determined to go to one of these places and spend a half hour with God.

The time arrives, you have made a space in your schedule around school or work, and so you go and sit down. Then you remember that you have one more quick call to make. Or maybe you left the stereo on. So you go and take care of that problem. Upon returning to your prayer space, you realize that your clothes are not really comfortable enough, and you are sure that if you just put on those comfy sweats, everything will be fine. So you go and change.

When you finally return you feel unsettled, and so you think that you should read some scripture before you begin to pray—just to get your mind in the proper place. After spending a few minutes deciding what scripture to read, you find a passage that seems appropriate and read it. Then your cell phone rings. Even though you have an answering feature, you just can't quite resist the urge to pick up the phone and see who is there.

After a ten-minute conversation, you feel wound up and distracted. You realize you need to do a lot that day. Looking at the clock, you see that twenty-five of your thirty minutes have passed. Telling yourself that this was

NOTE: The appendix offers step-by-step instructions for practicing solitude and silence individually or with a group.

not the right time to pray, you vow to try again later that evening and, turning your attention to the tasks before you, you head off into the rest of your day.

Prayer is difficult. It is not the techniques that are hard—most of the techniques are amusingly easy. Rather the difficulty lies in following through on the commitment to pray in the face of distractions that bear down on us or pick at us like annoying bugs, driving us away from the presence of God.

Our task is made even more difficult by the most obvious fact about the divine, a fact children constantly point out to the distress of the adults at church: We cannot see God. God is not visible and present the way a tree is, the way another person is, even the way our to-do list is. This fact leads to creating and worshiping idols; we want something tangible to see and feel and hold. When the people of Israel no longer saw the pillar of fire, when Moses was gone up the mountain and they were alone and afraid, the golden calf provided some small sense of security and hope, even if it was just metal (Exod. 32:1-6).

If therefore, we are ever going to pray, we need a way to counter these difficulties, these challenges that face us as we consider bringing ourselves before God. That way is the practice of listening, cultivated in the garden of silence and solitude. This ability to listen for God is the skill at the heart of the practice of prayer.

GOING OUT INTO THE DESERT

In the early days of the church, many Christians, perhaps most, believed that Jesus would return in their lifetime.

They believed that it would not be long before they would once again see God. The kingdom, God's reign, was coming. This hope gave the believers great strength and courage.

As the years went by, however, this notion started to fade. Church members began to die. The years dragged by and Jesus did not appear. People realized that they were in for a longer haul. As this realization dawned and took hold, people became increasingly aware of the distractions of the world, of the difficulties faced by all who would seek the mind of Christ. As this understanding grew, many in Palestine and Egypt pursued an unusual course of action: They went out into the desert to find God. Eventually these people became those we know as the desert mothers and fathers. They realized that in order to find God, in order to pray and realize the experience of salvation here and now, they needed to seek solitude and silence.

The gifts of these desert pray-ers to us are contained in groups of sayings and stories about their lives. From these resources we can see that they faced all of the same difficulties with prayer that we face. They were distracted. They wanted to do things, get work done. They were tempted to wander about in search of the perfect place to pray. The collected sayings became a counter to these temptations, a book of instruction and encouragement for those who were called to this difficult life.

> Abbot Anthony said: Just as fish die if they remain on dry land so monks, remaining away from their cells [the small caves or huts used by the desert pray-ers], or dwelling with men of the world, lose their determination to persevere in solitary prayer. Therefore, just as the fish should go back to the sea, so

we must return to our cells, lest remaining outside we forget to watch over ourselves interiorly. (*Wisdom of the Desert*, 29)

These words of encouragement convey a consistent and clear message: If you desire to seek the presence of God in your life, be silent and rest in prayer. Only through this interior quiet can you truly listen for Jesus.

GOD AT THE CENTER

Why is silence necessary for listening, and what happens when we enter into the silence of solitary prayer? We begin to let go of ourselves, which allows us to hear God. God is very gracious and patient. God does not usually interrupt us or push rudely into our affairs. If we choose to ignore God, God allows that. Such is the humility of a God who died on a cross. Therefore, if we wish to pray—and by this I mean open ourselves up to the possibility that God will speak to us, teach us, transform us—we must allow space in the busy world we have created. Like the ones who went into the desert, we must go to a place where the world does not overwhelm us.

When we go to sit in silence, when we turn our minds to our Creator, we begin the process of allowing God to be the center of our world. Usually we occupy that central position. We control the pace and tempo of our lives; we set the agenda; we decide what happens when. The practice of solitude turns this order of things upside down. Suddenly nothing is before us but empty space and time—no list of activities and chores, nothing important on our agenda. We place ourselves at God's disposal and we don't know when, or even if, our Creator will appear. This is unnerving.

We are not used to such a humble posture, especially if we are competent and successful people. How dare God keep us waiting! It must not be the right time, the right place. "My back hurts today, so I cannot really concentrate." The wisdom of the desert undermines such thinking.

A brother came to Abbot Pastor and said: Many distracting thoughts come into my mind, and I am in danger because of them. Then the elder thrust him out into the open air and said: Open up the garments about your chest and catch the wind in them. But he replied: This I cannot do. So the elder said to him: If you cannot catch the wind, neither can you prevent distracting thoughts from coming into your head. Your job is to say No to them. (*Wisdom of the Desert*, 43)

The work of silence is the work of gently saying no to the endless stream of thoughts and feelings that make up our world in order to listen for and say yes to the thoughts and feelings that are the voice of God. But how do we tell the difference? That discernment comes from practice. Because we cannot see God, we cannot easily tell which desires God places on our hearts and which arise from our own selfish wants. This potential confusion requires us to cultivate the skill of listening, the ground of all the practices described in this book. As we begin to work with and use these practices, we slowly begin to hear God over the chattering of our own internal dialogue.

LEARNING TO LISTEN

At one point in my prayer journey, I decided that I was going to sit on top of a hill for three days. I wasn't going to bring any food, just some water and a sleeping bag. No tent, no books, nothing to write with. I was going to spend time in solitude and silence; of course, God was going to show up immediately and talk to me.

So I set off. It was a three-mile hike from the parking lot to the top of the hill, and I began the journey with great enthusiasm and vigor. I was so excited that I would soon be talking with God!

When I finally reached the top I sat down, placed my sleeping bag and bottle of water beside me, and began to pray. Nothing happened. Soon my legs began to fall asleep, and my back got stiff. I was thinking about all sorts of things other than God, especially about how much time had passed. After I couldn't take it anymore, I allowed myself to look at the little clock I had brought with me— twenty minutes had gone by. No God, no revelations, a sore back, and two days, twenty-three hours, forty minutes to go.

I began to laugh. In that moment, many of my ideas about prayer and who I was as a pray-er crumbled to the ground. Prayer was obviously not something I could "do"; it wasn't something I could make happen or force or cause to come into existence. God created me; I did not make God; therefore, I could not cause God to speak when I wanted God to speak. I had to listen, and that meant not knowing what I would hear or when I would hear it.

I did stay on the hill for those three days. No voices, no great theophanies (actually seeing or hearing God directly). But I did learn something about listening and about how to listen: listening through all the distractions and habits of my own mind; listening even when I didn't want to listen—when my body ached, when it wasn't a good time, when no one would talk to me. One of the things I learned was that if I was faithful in my prayer, if I prayed even when it seemed futile, then eventually I would begin to notice that God is present.

This lesson is what the desert mothers and fathers discovered and what they speak to us down through the centuries: If they hung in there—stayed in their cells and kept praying even when assaulted by "demons" and battered by distractions—eventually Jesus would enter their hearts and minds, and his saving grace would transform them. They would hear his words to them; God would write a new law upon their hearts (Jer. 31:33).

FINDING OPPORTUNITIES FOR SILENCE

How does one practice solitude and silence? Are we all called to go into the desert alone or to sit up on the top of a hill? No, we are not; nor are such actions necessary for the practice of silence. However, as we observed in this chapter's opening scenario, silence challenges us; entering into silence does require a certain amount of discipline and commitment. As mentioned above, silence and solitude are the basis for all the prayer practices we are exploring. Thus the ability to rest in silence is both required for the practices and strengthened by them.

One of the best ways to begin practicing solitude is to notice times when silence occurs naturally in our day. Even those of us who are incredibly busy have moments when we are alone, when nothing is happening. Usually we ignore these moments or find ways to fill them. Instead, we can appreciate these times and savor them. We can use these times to turn inward and attend to our feelings.

Time in the car offers an excellent example of a potential period of silence. Although we need to attend to our driving, this is a time when we can actually be both alone and quiet. Usually we fill this time with listening to music or talking on the phone. Next time you drive, try something different. Don't turn on any gadgets. Tell God that you intend to use this time to pray, to just be quiet. Then see what happens. Watch the thoughts and feelings that arise. Notice your own distractions. What is the state of your mind, your heart? Are you at peace? Are you angry, sad, confused? Have you thought about God yet that day? When you arrive at your destination, thank God for the time together, whatever has happened. Don't berate yourself if you haven't had a "good" experience. You can try again.

You also might try this exercise at several different times during the day. Once you begin to ask these questions and notice the answers, you cultivate a sense of curiosity about your inner life. You start to listen to the state of your being. Sinking into the still waters to drink from the pool of God's care becomes permissible. Silence becomes not an enemy but a welcome guest. As you make friends with silence, noticing opportunities for practicing it becomes easier.

Going Deeper into the Silence

Maybe you already enjoy silence. You like quiet times alone and relish those moments when your thoughts and feelings belong only to you. If so, then perhaps this comfort presents an invitation to go deeper into the silence, to spend more time in prayer, to cultivate another prayer practice.

You may experience this call to depth as a greater longing for prayer. You find that setting aside time to pray seems easier. Or perhaps you notice an advertisement for a retreat on prayer and find you have time to attend. These are callings from God, drawing you into the divine Presence. Heed them; be grateful for them.

Either way—whether silence comes naturally or is a challenge—every one of us can continue to work on our listening. We can allow God to open us more and more to the wonder of the kingdom of God, that sacred world toward which Jesus beckons us.

PRACTICING SILENCE IN GROUPS

This mention of the kingdom—that ancient notion of a society in which the rule of divine Love reigns supreme—raises the question of community. What about my church? What about my Sunday school class, Bible study, or covenant group? If silence and solitude are so essential to prayer, where does the group fit in?

As in our individual lives, we miss opportunities to practice silence in groups. For example, times of silence could be built into any group meeting. A group might decide to practice silence during a meal. Another possible time for silence is during a bus ride together. Rather than talking, listening to CDs, or watching a movie, a group could covenant to spend the trip in silence.

Paradoxically, the more the desert mothers and fathers sought out silence, the more people sought them out. Whole cities grew up near their caves, prompting some monks to build barricades across their cell entrances. Yet still people would come to them for advice and spiritual guidance. They came for two major reasons. First, the spiritual power of these desert mothers and fathers drew those seeking salvation to them. For God's imperative that the fruits of prayer and salvation be shared with a world in desperate need of Jesus' love overshadowed the desert pray-ers' own inclination to solitude. Second, people needed help in their spiritual journey. It is hard to go it alone. In similar fashion, groups and others who are on "the Way" naturally seek out one another for comfort, help, and support.

A group can function in several ways relative to silence and solitude. First of all, it is possible to pray in silence together, as the previous examples demonstrate. People who have prayed in groups over long periods realize that a connection and sense of support develop, even though group members experience little or no verbal interaction. I once went on a retreat with forty people, and we spent the first two weeks in silence. At the end of that time I was amazed to realize we felt closer to one another even though we had not spoken a word. This closeness forms because as we enter into silence together, we begin to connect to the one God, the one Spirit that flows in, through, and between us all.

Second, a group can function as a place to share the experience of silence and get feedback. For example, if a group decides to spend a meal in silence, then afterward members may take time to reflect together about the experience. This sharing time can be rich and rewarding as people express their insights from the prayer. Communicating the thoughts and feelings that arise in the silence often helps clarify what is happening in our own prayer life.

Finally, a group can support and encourage us on our journey. When we enter dry times, or the path seems to disappear, or God feels far away, a group of faithful travelers with whom to share our suffering is important. Often another's word will keep us from running from our prayer.

The sharing is a time of listening and supportive feedback. Avoid a situation in which members try to fix or give advice to the person sharing. Also it is essential for the leader to have significant experience in the chosen prayer practice. I will say more about the group process in later chapters. The wisdom of the desert affirms the value of the group for spiritual life:

> The same Father said: If there are three monks living together, of whom one remains silent in prayer at all times, and another is ailing and gives thanks for it, and the third waits on them both with sincere good will, these three are equal, as if they were performing the same work. (*Wisdom of the Desert,* 42–43)

With this first chapter the journey of prayer has begun. Silence and solitude, the practices that promote a holy listening, lie at the heart of this journey, which can both challenge us and bring us joy and excitement. The words of the desert echo through the centuries:

> Abbot Lot came to Abbot Joseph and said: Father, according as I am able, I keep my little rule, and my little fast, my prayer, meditation and contemplative silence; and according as I am able I strive to cleanse my heart of thoughts: now what more should I do? The elder rose up in reply and stretched out his hands to heaven, and his fingers became like ten lamps of fire. He said: Why not be totally changed into fire? (*Wisdom of the Desert,* 50)

TWO

LECTIO DIVINA
Encountering Scripture through Sacred Reading

TRAVELING COMPANION
Saint Benedict

*Sacred reading is a
living conversation between you and God.*

ny trip we take requires a guide. Many of us, before we set off in our car, first log on to the Internet to get maps and driving directions so that we know how to get where we are going. The need for direction is no less in the spiritual journey. Silence and solitude are wonderful, but without a map they can take us on a descent into the nightmare of our own delusions and fantasies; that is, we can fully encounter our fallen selves.

And so in this chapter we come to the Bible, that wonderful and mysterious book that speaks to us of God. Yet how do we allow the Bible to be our guide? Reading the Bible and praying the Bible are two very different undertakings. To pray the Bible is to apply listening and silence to the Word of God in order to hear God speak. This chapter will explore the practice of *lectio divina,* the sacred reading of scripture.

Imagine that you own only one book. For most of us, this scenario may be too unreal even to contemplate. Yet throughout the course of human history, having even one book in a home has been exceptional. Now try to imagine how you might relate to that single volume. At first you might read it fairly quickly, just as you would read any book today. Then you realize you have read your only book; you cannot throw that one out and pick up another. Maybe you give up reading for a few weeks. Soon, however, you are drawn back to your book. You want to read. Somehow the words on the page connect you with something outside yourself, a greater world.

NOTE: The appendix offers step-by-step instructions for practicing *lectio divina* individually or with a group.

The ancient Hebrews believed writing had a similar sacred power. They regarded words and letters as instruments for connecting readers to something beyond people's own circumstances. To the Hebrews it seemed miraculous that simple lines of ink could suddenly become sources of knowledge and information.

Let's go back to your book. Maybe you read one chapter, noting with some lament that you remember it quite well, and it is not really new and exciting anymore. As you start rereading the second chapter, however, suddenly one sentence catches your attention, a detail you had not remembered. Furthermore, this small scrap of the story reminds you of something in your own life—something that happened years ago and ended unresolved or perhaps a dilemma with friends or parents. You find yourself transported back in time. You are no longer reading; rather you are listening to your inner voice, your memory, your imagination. You are in relationship with your younger self and the people you knew long ago. Perhaps this journey encourages you to contact an old friend, to heal an old wound, or just to savor a wonderful memory.

When this imaginary trip is over, you return to your book with renewed vigor and excitement. You realize that this simple volume contains doors to hundreds of worlds. It is a machine for traveling through time and space, a portal into your self and into lives you have lived and might live. What you first considered "just a book" you now regard with awe.

The ancients realized that scripture, when read the right way, opens doors to a direct relationship with God. They discovered the prayer of sacred reading. Today we generally have lost this understanding of reading. We read in a mechanical, consumer-oriented manner. We read to acquire information, to get what we want out of a book, and then we leave it disregarded on a shelf. Even the Bible has fallen prey to our carnivorous reading habits. We read the Bible to get religious information, to get "right answers," to confirm our own ideas about God, to supply us with weapons in our petty wars over doctrine and institutional law, to find support for our arguments with friends or foes. We force the Bible to conform to our own views rather than allowing the Bible to form us into God's people. This is not the only way to read scripture.

Saint Benedict and Sacred Reading

Sometime after 500 C.E. an Italian we now know as Saint Benedict gathered a group of ordinary people into a community, which would be called a monastery. As with many of our traveling companions, we do not know a lot about Benedict the person. He stood in awe of the desert mothers and fathers as people who truly lived a life designed to realize the mind of Christ. Yet he also seems to have understood that the life of solitary prayer would not work for most people. Instead individuals needed a stable spiritual community in order to advance in the life of faith.

To guide his community, Benedict wrote a rule, a set of guidelines for the common life and spiritual practice of the members. The purpose of the *Rule* was to help create a "school for the service of the Lord," a place where people could come and learn how to be with Jesus (*Rule*, 5).

One of the three primary tools of this school was reading; the other two were liturgical prayer and work. Yet this was not the kind of reading we know today. Rather, Benedict prescribed *lectio divina,* sacred reading, a prayer practice designed to cultivate contemplative listening. For it was through such listening that the monks could become aware of the presence of the Holy Spirit in their hearts and minds.

Benedict's monks did not own even one book. Most of them probably were illiterate; they "read" by being read to. They would listen to the words of scripture, memorize them, and then "read" them back to themselves, sometimes for up to six hours a day.

This process of reading takes seriously the notion that the Bible is the living Word of God. Through the Bible, God can actually speak to the reader directly, now, in real time. What is required in order to hear God's voice is a practice that teaches the believer how to "incline the ear of your heart" (*Rule,* 1). In order to do this Benedict wanted the monks to ruminate on—literally to "chew" or "digest"—the Word of God, much as a cow would chew its cud. This practice became a staple of monastic life for fifteen hundred years and is handed to us as a gift from the distant past.

STEPS IN A LIVING CONVERSATION

Lectio divina, as a formal prayer practice, consists of four steps or phases. These steps are not mechanical activities you must perform correctly in a certain order to "get it right." Sacred reading is a living conversation between you and God. In the same way that conversation with another person has rhythms, ebbs, and flows, so too does sacred reading. If we are talking with our best friend and constantly interrupt or, at the other extreme, never say anything, then the conversation will have little value. A rich, lively conversation encompasses times of listening and times of responding, times of speech and times of silence. Think of the waves upon the shore; they break with tremendous force and noise; they gurgle up to the shore, and then silently recede. Such is the rhythm of *lectio divina.*

Still it is helpful to distinguish four phases of the prayer: *lectio* (listening/reading), *meditatio* (meditation), *oratio* (prayer), *contemplatio* (contemplation). The implementation of these phases depends on whether you are doing sacred reading alone or with a group. I will begin by describing the process for an individual and then move on to the process for a group.

Lectio

The key to *lectio divina* is not focusing too much on the literal, surface meaning of the passage you are reading. That meaning may end up being important, but it is also quite possible that God will use the passage to speak to you about something completely unrelated to its literal content.

You begin by selecting a passage and reading it to yourself. If you are not sure where to start, you might try a favorite psalm or a story in one of the Gospels or any of the following passages in Isaiah: 40:1-8; 43:1-7; 44:1-5; or 49:1-6. Read the passage several times. As you read, allow the words to sink down into the depths of your being. Allow your body and mind to become a deep cavern in which the Word of God echoes, bouncing off the walls of the cave and slowly disappearing into the shadows of your mind. Imagine the first monks in Benedict's abbey, huddled together in the candlelight, listening to the words of the psalmist repeated again and again until they became like old friends, speaking truth and wisdom.

This process of reading then gives way to listening. Listening for what? At this stage you are listening for a word or phrase from the passage that stands out for you, one that catches your attention over all the others. A hyperlink on the Internet is a modern metaphor for this process. You are reading an article at your favorite Web site when you come across a phrase highlighted in blue. If you were to click on this phrase, you would jump to another site. You pause to consider whether or not to go there. Has the phrase caught your interest? Do you want to find out more about this particular topic? This type of reflection is the nature of *lectio*. As you mull over the words and phrases of your passage, listen for the hypertext. Listen for those words that tug at you, that invite you to go deeper into the mystery of God. God is calling to you through the text; deep is calling to deep as God speaks to the image of God buried inside you. Which words of your passage call out to you?

As you hear that call, focus your attention on the word or phrase. Begin to repeat it to yourself; sit with the word, listen to it, and allow it to resonate within you. Let the word draw you into the next phase of the prayer.

Meditatio

In this next phase you begin to meditate upon your word, the one that has caught your attention and is drawing you into deeper relationship with God. Following our Internet metaphor, this is the hyperlink you have chosen; you click on it and now you are at a new Web site. You have left the confines of your original passage, and you are floating freely in spiritual cyberspace. God can take you anywhere.

So allow your heart and mind to follow your word. What images come to mind? What thoughts, what feelings? Perhaps a particular memory is stirred, an unresolved situation in your life or something in need of healing, in need of Christ's touch. Or maybe you see an imaginary scene; you are out in a field or in your favorite church. God has something to say to you.

In Benedict's time, the great masters felt that when a disciple came to them with a problem, the solution was not a lengthy piece of advice but rather "a word." God had something particular to say to the disciple, and it was up to the master to listen with enough clarity to know and then speak the word needed for that person to be healed. This process lies at the heart of *lectio divina;* Jesus has heard your prayer and seeks to speak to you exactly that which you need to hear through your word. In this phase of the prayer, you allow your mind the freedom to follow faithfully as you seek the voice of God.

As you come across these images, thoughts, and feelings, savor them; repeat your word and allow yourself to listen. At some point in this process, you may find yourself wanting to speak to God, a desire that signals the next phase of the prayer.

Oratio

Any good conversation consists of both listening and speaking. In a natural rhythm—a dance—both partners move and respond to each other in time to the music. This is no less true of the process of prayer. After a time of listening to God in the stillness, we are moved to respond. Yet we must remember not to do this too quickly or impulsively. Wait for the words to arise from deep within.

As you wait, let yourself be aware of what you most desire to say to God. Perhaps you have wandered into a long-forgotten memory, and you need to ask why God has shown this to you. Or maybe you have been asked to look at some pain you have caused another, and you begin to wonder how you can seek forgiveness. Maybe God has shown you a time of great joy, and you simply want to express your gratitude. Whatever you desire to speak, allow your voice to be clear and use few words. In silence speak your prayer to God.

The movement from *lectio* through *oratio* is a conversation, the ebb and flow of *lectio divina:* Your original passage is God's Word; you pick the word that stirs you; God guides you to new places; you speak with God of the new desires that these places stir in you. This process allows you to cultivate an awareness of the Spirit's presence within. In the silence of the prayer, the Holy Spirit is given room to speak, and as you listen you are guided toward what God places upon your heart. The Word of God becomes real and alive and active in you right here, right now.

You speak to God and then you return to the posture of one who listens. You go back to your word or your images and allow God to answer you anew. For Benedict this process was not merely circular. Benedict and the ancient monks viewed *lectio divina* as similar to Jacob's ladder (Gen. 28:12), a spiral stair by which they might ascend to heaven. So allow yourself to climb. When you are ready to rest, you have come to the final phase of the process.

Contemplatio

Every conversation eventually comes to an end. At some point there is a conclusion or a need to rest. Perhaps your allotted time for prayer has ended, or maybe you just notice that the prayer journey has come to a close. You have enough new information; you need to rest in the stillness and examine your new view of the world; or God knows that you can absorb no more. You experience a feeling of completion, a deeper silence that you no longer wish to move out of: You have nothing left to say, and God too has fallen silent. This is the moment of contemplative rest.

This resting moment offers a time to look back over the whole of the prayer experience. It is a landing on the staircase to heaven. Look at your new view of the world, at your new view of yourself and God. Maybe this new view contains answers, a new direction, or something concrete to respond to; or, maybe you are left with new questions. Either way, God has spoken to you, and this is something to be grateful for.

Saint Benedict told the monks to express their gratitude to God for encountering the living Word during this final phase of the prayer. This gratitude may be acknowledged with a simple "thank you." If God has called you to a particular action, ask for God's blessing as you commit yourself to this new direction in your life.

There is another possible conclusion to your prayer. Perhaps you have heard nothing. You may feel frustrated and angry because all you thought about during your prayer time was your shopping list or your job or something else seemingly unrelated to God. The server was down; the Internet crashed; all the links were inactive.

For those of us who have grown up in a society that places ultimate value on "getting things done," the experience of "nothing happening" is maddening. However, from Benedict's perspective, such "failure" is a normal part of our fallen human condition. If encountering God's Word were easy, there would be no need to practice prayer! Prayer is not a product; it is a relationship. Even if you did not experience the wonderful event you imagined, God knows your intention. You wanted to spend time with Jesus, and in some way, although exactly how is a mystery to you, you did. So express your frustration to God; ask for help and for the strength to try again. God does not require that we be successful, just faithful.

LECTIO DIVINA IN A GROUP SETTING

Lectio divina is a wonderful prayer practice for a group setting. The basic format of the prayer can be adjusted in many ways to fit the size, length of time, and experience level of the group involved. Numerous church communities around the world are incorporating inventive ways to practice *lectio divina* in the regular life of the community.

The main difference between the individual practice and the group practice is that group participants speak their "noticings" aloud for the group to hear how God is speaking to each person. A group may use four phases, as individuals do; or, it may employ one, two, or three phases, depending on the time and inclination of group members. Here I will outline both the two- and three-phase processes. I use the former at a small morning-prayer group at our church and the latter in longer, retreat settings. The two-phase process uses the *lectio* and *oratio* steps; the three-phase process adds the *meditatio* step between these two.

Begin the practice by reading the selected passage of scripture aloud twice (these two readings together are considered the "first reading"). Ask participants to notice the word or phrase from the passage that stands out for them as they listen to the two readings. After a minute or two of silence, invite participants to share that word or phrase with the other group members without commentary.

Then, following more silence, read the passage a third time (the "second reading") and allow for more silence. In the two-phase process, let participants move to the *oratio* step and invite them to listen in the silence for how God is speaking to them through the passage. God's voice may present itself in the form of questions, observations, images, thoughts, or feelings. Many longtime churchgoers may find it difficult at this stage simply to listen for the unique voice of God, speaking to them right then and there—and to refrain from asking, "What is the correct meaning of this passage?" Then, after the silent time of one or two minutes, ask members of the group to share the fruit of their listening with the group.

In the three-phase process, *meditatio* follows the second reading of the passage. During this reflection time, encourage participants to notice any images that are given to them in the silence. After the silence, the participants share their images, which may be abstract or concrete, visual or verbal. For example, in one prayer time with a group of local pastors, I was leading *lectio divina* using the story of Samuel's calling (1 Sam. 3). During the second phase *(meditatio),* the members of the group shared such images as "a long hallway with a single door at the end," "I remember my ordination," and "standing outside the church in the dark."

For the three-phase process, read the passage a third time. In the silence following that reading, group members may listen for how God is speaking to them through the passage *(oratio)*. This "speaking" can come in various forms. Individuals may be conscious of an observation, may sense an ethical imperative or a call to action, may feel a form of assurance or a validation of God's presence, or they may experience the vast silence that is also the voice of God.

No matter which form of the group practice you use, encouraging the group members to listen is the key. The leader's role is to help people understand that the practice of *lectio* is not about comprehending the passage intellectually but rather cultivating awareness of the Holy Spirit's speaking to them through scripture.

The monastics who follow Benedict's *Rule* have practiced this way of reading scripture for centuries and still do to this day. Sitting alone in their cells or sitting together at meals, they listen to the Bible again and again and allow themselves to be formed by the Word. This spiritual formation through listening is the heart of *lectio divina*.

THREE

THE JESUS PRAYER
There Is Power in His Name

*When we look at how the pilgrim
put the Jesus Prayer at the center of his life
and allowed this prayer to lead and
transform him, we see a wonderful example
of how a prayer practice can,
over time, come to create a life with God.*

*J*esus Christ, Son of God, have mercy on me."

Silence, solitude, praying with scripture—this book could end right here. These three things are at the heart of all contemplative prayer. They are all the practices one needs to live a life with God. However, in the same way God did not create just one kind of plant or animal, God did not gift us with just one type of prayer practice.

We each have different ways of understanding and viewing the world around us. Some people see in images; some hear words; some speak with silence; and some long to move their bodies to the unseen rhythms of the Holy Spirit. These differences are to be celebrated, as together they give us a full and glorious picture of the miraculous tapestry that is the mind and body of Christ. Because of these differences, God has gifted us with a variety of prayer practices, each allowing us to speak with the one God, albeit through diverse aspects of our being.

"Jesus Christ, Son of God, have mercy on me."

Silence, solitude, and sacred reading may make up the bedrock, the foundation, of all prayer practices, yet from that ground spring many other modes of praying. The next five chapters will explore practices that focus on the heart and mind of the one who prays. Now this focus does not mean that the body is not involved; nor does it imply that exterior relationships are not important in these practices. The dominant emphasis of the practices is simply on the mind and heart.

"Jesus Christ, Son of God, have mercy on me."

NOTE: The appendix offers step-by-step instructions for practicing the Jesus Prayer individually or with a group.

What do I mean by the mind and heart? The answer to that question could be the subject of a separate book, but for the sake of simplicity I mean all that is contained within the processes of thought and emotion. This includes our ideas, thoughts, memories, feelings, and other sensory input—all the content of our interior psychic space. In these prayer practices, this content becomes the focus of the prayer. The thousands of separate shreds of mental events are sifted, sorted, and caressed until they settle into a fertile pile of that good soil from which grows the Word of God. The first of these practices, which I take up in this chapter, is the Jesus Prayer; the constant repetition of the phrase "Jesus Christ, Son of David [or God], have mercy on me [a sinner]."

In order to understand the Jesus Prayer, we begin with the scripture that contains these phrases. Blind Bartimaeus stands by the side of the road and cries, "Jesus, Son of David, have mercy on me!" (Mark 10:47). The blind man cries out to Jesus from the darkness of his existence, hoping, with a fervent power that overcomes any hesitancy, that Jesus will hear and respond.

"Jesus Christ, Son of God, have mercy on me."

As I mentioned earlier, people in biblical times had an appreciation for the power of words that we have all but lost. In *lectio divina,* the power of the word is the possibility that God may speak directly to the one who prays the word. In the Jesus Prayer, the power of the word is the ability to create a new human being in the person praying.

Try to imagine yourself a human at the dawn of time. There are no written words, no books, no copy machines, no faxes or e-mails. You scratch out your existence on the land, living with your tribe. Then one day someone shows you something amazing. It is a small piece of dried reed bearing small black marks. This seems of no account to you until the person tells you that these markings are words! This person then explains what the words are; he or she reads to you and out of thin air is able to create a whole world of meaning.

No, you think, *this isn't possible. How could such marks actually contain so much meaning?* Deriving meaning from markings on a piece of reed would seem like magic to you. Indeed our spiritual ancestors came to associate this "magic" with the act of creation itself. Words contained meaning, and meaning gave life to an abstract symbol or idea. Thus God spoke words and the world came into existence. Given this connection of the word with creation, naming came to be seen as a powerful act; if one could ascribe a name to something, then one understood its essence—the thought that created the being. Awe for the power of naming underlies the Hebrews' practice of never speaking the name of God: No one is capable of understanding the essence of the divine.

"Jesus Christ, Son of God, have mercy on me."

With this background, we can recognize the power of the blind man's cry. By naming Jesus from inside his darkness, the blind man recognizes the power of God to change his life; he knows that as his cry echoes back to him, it will transform him. Indeed this is what happens. Jesus calls the blind man over and tells him that his faith has made him well; suddenly the man can see. It is from this story in scripture, as well as from the view that the name of God contains tremendous power in and of itself, that the Jesus Prayer emerges.

"Jesus Christ, Son of God, have mercy on me."

Exactly when the Jesus Prayer began is unknown. Probably the prayer did not start in any one place and time. However, it has been most popular within the monasteries of the Eastern Church (what we now call the Orthodox Church). In more modern times, the prayer became widely known through the publication of a manuscript written by an unknown Russian sometime in the late nineteenth century. This book, *The Way of a Pilgrim*, brought the Jesus Prayer out from the monastic enclosure and into the world.

THE PILGRIM

The pilgrim's journey is initiated by an encounter with scripture: "I went to church . . . , and among other words I heard these—'Pray without ceasing.' It was this text, more than any other, which forced itself upon my mind" (*Way of a Pilgrim*, 3). This phrase stands out for this simple man and works its way into his consciousness to such a degree that it soon defines his life.

He begins to try to understand how this praying without ceasing is possible. He goes to church, but (and this may sound familiar to you too) he finds that the pastors have nothing to say about prayer. He asks many people, but none can help him. Finally he encounters one of the *startsi*. This Russian word means "experienced elders" or spiritual directors—persons who guide others in developing their relationship with God. This man gives our seeker the following instructions:

The continuous interior prayer of Jesus is a constant uninterrupted calling upon the divine name of Jesus with the lips, in the spirit, in the heart, while forming a mental picture of His constant presence, and imploring His grace, during every occupation, at all times, in all places, even during sleep. The appeal is couched in these terms, "Lord Jesus Christ, have mercy on me." (*Way of a Pilgrim*, 9)

"Jesus Christ, Son of God, have mercy on me."

The pray-er of the Jesus Prayer is to cry out to God in a continuous manner, like blind Bartimaeus, against all odds and distractions and ignoring any who say to be quiet. The pilgrim receives this instruction from his director. So, armed with the Jesus Prayer and a volume of the mystical theology of the Russian church fathers, he sets out, walking the highways and byways, determined to discover the results of praying without ceasing.

What he finds is most amazing. At first the prayer is hard for him. He cannot manage to concentrate on the words and soon becomes lost in his own thoughts and preoccupations. However as time goes on, the prayer becomes more and more a part of his thoughts until he is saying it continuously. Soon he begins to experience the transforming power of God.

When about three weeks had passed I felt a pain in my heart, and then a most delightful warmth, as well as consolation and peace. This aroused me still more . . . to give great care to the saying of the prayer so that all my thoughts were taken up with it and I felt a very great joy. (*Way of a Pilgrim*, 38)

"Jesus Christ, Son of God, have mercy on me."

A number of elements in Christian tradition encourage the practice of speaking a word or phrase repetitively. One of the best examples is the Lord's Prayer, which Christians pray at some point during almost every worship service. Other examples include the word *amen* and the repetitive use of the psalms in many different Christian communities. This type of practice, if performed in an attitude of prayer as opposed to a mechanical repetition with little awareness of the content, develops the skill of contemplative concentration—focusing the mind upon a single point.

Imagine that the world as we know it, the sinful world separated from God, is like a giant sheet of blank paper extending to infinity in all directions. This paper stands directly in front of us and on it we paint the picture of our lives. The painting process enthralls us to the point of losing ourselves and forgetting to search for God. The practice of the repetitive prayer acts like a magnifying glass held up to the sunlight: It focuses an intense beam of spiritual energy on one point of the page, which then slowly burns a hole in the paper. At some point our concentration propels us through this hole, and we "pop out" to the other side—into the kingdom of God.

At some point in the pilgrim's prayer experience, he is transformed into a person who lives in another space—the space of the present reign of God. Once this transformation has occurred, no matter what happens to him, he responds to life in ways that both amaze and confuse those around him. When he is robbed and beaten, he responds with joy. When he is offered shelter and companionship, he says he would rather walk in the snow and pray. While he says he is a common man, people think they are talking to a learned saint. As the prayer touched his heart on the inside, his whole being had been transformed so that even his outer appearance changed. This transformation is the "fruit of the Spirit" Paul describes (Gal. 5:22-23). When people are amazed, the pilgrim responds simply:

> It costs nothing but the effort to sink down in silence into the depths of one's heart and call more and more upon the radiant name of Jesus. Everyone who does that feels at once the inward light, everything becomes understandable to him, he even catches sight in this light of some of the mysteries of the kingdom of God. (*Way of a Pilgrim*, 78)

Following the passage of scripture that caught his attention led the pilgrim eventually to learn the Jesus Prayer. This prayer combines silence and scripture into one practice. When we look at the pilgrim putting the Jesus Prayer at the center of his life and allowing this prayer to lead and transform him, we see a wonderful example of how a prayer practice can, over time, create a life with God.

"Jesus Christ, Son of God, have mercy on me."

So how to do this? Well, our pilgrim friend tells us that it's easy. (Yet if it really were so easy, there would be more Christians practicing these sorts of prayers.) In reality, praying the Jesus Prayer is very challenging.

PRAYING THE JESUS PRAYER

The practice itself is simple: Repeat silently again and again the phrase "Jesus Christ, Son of God, have mercy on me." (There are minor variations on this phrase as we read in the pilgrim's description. Pick a variation that sounds comfortable for you; the exact wording, so long as it contains the name of Jesus, is irrelevant.) That's it.

"Jesus Christ, Son of God, have mercy on me."

Now comes the challenge. What do we do with the distractions? What do we do when our mind wanders? What do we do when we realize we stopped saying the prayer fifteen minutes ago and we've been thinking about friends or a conflict with the boss? We just go back to repeating the prayer. The pilgrim reports these same problems. He simply returns to his one-pointed concentration. At first bypassing distractions is hard, but the more he does it, the easier it becomes.

"Jesus Christ, Son of God, have mercy on me."

Why is this concentration so challenging?

The trouble is that we live far from ourselves and have but little wish to get any nearer to ourselves. Indeed we are running away all the time to avoid coming face to face with our real selves, and we barter the truth for trifles. (*Way of a Pilgrim*, 79)

Here our wise pilgrim speaks to the central problem of the contemplative life. When we enter the realm of our hearts and minds through a prayer such as the Jesus Prayer, we first encounter ourselves. We see our fears, our hatreds, our petty concerns, our self-centered preoccupations, our wounds. It is often not a pretty sight.

"Jesus Christ, Son of God, have mercy on me."

So we run. We convince ourselves that the Jesus Prayer is not the right prayer; it's not the right time; the prayer is not truly Christian—anything to help us escape the pain of our own existence. At this point, the important thing is to keep trying. Go back to the prayer; use times of solitude, such as time in the car, given to you in your schedule.

When to Pray the Jesus Prayer

It is possible to pray the Jesus Prayer whenever you are alone or in silence with others. You might pray on a walk, in the car, on a bus, or when you are at home. You might begin with a short period of time, say, ten or fifteen minutes, and then try longer periods of time as you deepen the practice. After a while you may find yourself praying spontaneously, much like returning repeatedly to a song stuck in your head.

One of the best times for me to pray the Jesus Prayer is at night when I cannot sleep. Rather than tossing and turning and getting upset that I am still awake, I simply begin to pray the Jesus Prayer. Remember that the pilgrim was told to pray the prayer even in his sleep! Often I do fall asleep right away. The times when sleep comes more slowly are wonderful periods of prayer. In the deep silence of the night, I can lift my heart and mind to my Creator—a soft voice ringing out into the infinite.

"Jesus Christ, Son of God, have mercy on me."

The Jesus Prayer in Groups

What about the use of this prayer in groups? Although there are no spoken parts to the Jesus Prayer, it can be practiced in a group setting. Also, as with silence, discussion in a group after the prayer can be helpful for this practice.

Recently I incorporated the Jesus Prayer into a worship service at church. First I encouraged people to go off on their own and spend fifteen minutes praying. They were free to sit by themselves or walk as they prayed—whatever was comfortable for them. (If more convenient, everyone may remain in the same room, silently praying together.)

Following this prayer time, all gathered in groups of five or six and shared their experiences with one another.

The format of this sharing was simple: Each person took a few minutes to describe his or her own experience of prayer or of noticing God during the prayer time. The other members of the group listened without offering any interpretations, advice, or comments. These small-group sessions proved extremely valuable. For it was not only important for people to be able to share what happened to them, but it was almost more worthwhile for people to be able to hear what happened to others.

One of the most amazing accomplishments of the pilgrim is not what he did but the fact that he did it all on his own. For most of us, contemplative prayer is so challenging that we need the support of a group—a community—to help us through the difficulties, to encourage us to persevere. A group serves as a form of support and nourishment.

The sharing in the group time can validate our experience and help us to recognize we are not the only ones who struggle. If an ongoing established group, such as a class or a youth group, decides to do the Jesus Prayer regularly for a period of time, then the group serves as a wonderful place to watch the prayer's effects blossom over time.

The group serves another function as well. The pilgrim's solitary journey was impressive not only because he persevered but also because he did not lose his way and wander into delusion or madness. As you enter the world of deep prayer and are assaulted by your distractions and demons, it is possible to be seduced by a path that is not of God. One function of the group is to prevent this from happening, and that function makes it essential for the group leader (or worship leader if the groups are part of a worship gathering as in the example above) to have experience practicing the Jesus Prayer. Individuals should not try to teach or lead any of the prayers described in this book until they have experience practicing them. As one gains some knowledge of the prayer, its dynamics, and the obstacles that can occur as one prays, one is able to guide others. Without such understanding, the group experience can become a case of the blind leading the blind.

"Jesus Christ, Son of God, have mercy on me."

The pilgrim wanders down the road and disappears over the horizon. In his wake he leaves the echo of the Jesus Prayer ringing in our ears. He has given us a great gift, and he offers it to us for free, just as God pours out abundant grace for free. And just as the Jesus Prayer has accompanied us throughout this chapter, it is now up to us to take the gift beyond this book and use it in our travels.

"Jesus Christ, Son of God, have mercy on me."

FOUR

APOPHATIC PRAYER
Be Still and Know

*We must admit that we are helpless
before God. We must trust
that our Creator will come and find us.*

*W*ords are the primary vehicle for both *lectio divina* and the Jesus Prayer. By applying concentration and using imagery, repetition, and listening, the words and phrases that we encounter in these practices help us to seek God. But what if we were to go beyond the words? What if we entered into a place where there were no words, no guideposts, no landscape? Should this happen, we would arrive in the realm of apophatic prayer, the subject of this chapter.

Were I to be absolutely true to the nature of this prayer practice, all the pages of this chapter would be blank. Unfortunately I do not think that my publisher, nor many readers, would tolerate this. Yet such a demonstration of radical emptiness might be a more accurate explanation of this type of prayer than the few thousand words that follow. This is because apophatic prayer, or silent contemplative prayer (I will use these terms interchangeably within this chapter), is prayer without images. In this prayer we are drawn into that vast space that is God without words, names, concepts. In this prayer we begin to take seriously the comment, often made but not practiced, that God is beyond all that we know of God. "All the being of creation then, compared with the infinite Being of God, is nothing" (*Ascent of Mount Carmel*, 25).

Every time we read "LORD" in the Bible, we encounter this understanding of the nature of God. For this word is a translation of the Hebrew *YHWH*, a name of God that was never to be spoken. Yet even the Hebrews wrote *YHWH* rather than leave a blank space in their scripture, and in the

NOTE: The appendix offers step-by-step instructions for practicing apophatic prayer individually or with a group.

same way, I must try to say something about this type of prayer, the essence of which is nothing.

As with all our practices, this one undoubtedly has ancient roots. Then in fourteenth-century England, an unknown author penned a book titled *The Cloud of Unknowing*, which attempted to explain and describe silent contemplative prayer. This book, along with the works of Saint John of the Cross and of Saint Teresa of Ávila in sixteenth-century Spain, has helped to make apophatic prayer available to us today. (There are several modern versions of such prayer. One is Centering Prayer, made popular by Thomas Keating and Basil Pennington; another is Christian meditation as described by John Main.)

GOD'S SPACE: THE REALM OF PARADOX AND NONTHOUGHT

As we shall see, however, *available* does not mean *easy*. For people who are used to multitasking, linear thinking, and right/wrong answers, apophatic prayer is a recipe for insanity because this style of prayer relies upon and develops the contemplative skills of paradox and nonthought. What do I mean by these concepts?

Paradox is the practice of coming to understand a greater truth by simultaneously accepting two apparently opposing concepts. An example of a paradox is the idea that we can know God by not knowing anything about God. On the face of it, this does not make sense; yet it is nonsensical only to our normal way of understanding. If we look beyond linear logic, we can begin to see the truth in the statement, for we realize that if we let go of our own limited way of knowing, God can infuse a deeper knowing into our consciousness, and so we know God by not knowing.

Paradoxical statements are the "riddles" (Prov. 1:6) of the wisdom teachers, a reference echoed in the words of the person who penned *The Cloud of Unknowing* (referred to as "our author" from now on): "I do not choose to express the interior life in this way [a straightforward manner]. Rather I will speak in paradoxes" (*Cloud*, 136).

Nonthought is a closely related concept. We give up trying to understand through our usual logical thought process and allow God to do the thinking for us. Our unknown author of *The Cloud of Unknowing* is a master at these skills. For example, ask how to do silent prayer and the author answers, "If you ask me just precisely how one is to go about doing the contemplative work of love [silent prayer], I am at a complete loss" (*Cloud*, 90). We are back to the blank sheets of paper.

We live in a world where there are always things to do and always right or wrong answers. Whether for multiple-choice tests or tasks at work, we are told that a solution exists and an activity will fit the situation. There are good choices and bad choices; you can get either a good grade or a bad grade. There is a winner and a loser. Recently I heard a group of young people talking about how some got a "140" on a paper while others got "only a 139." We are trained to think like computers in a binary world of 0s and 1s; the switch is either on or off.

Apophatic prayer smashes these idols of exactitude and certainty. As we enter the contemplative silence that our author termed the "Cloud of Unknowing," we come to the realization that we know nothing of God; we must simply surrender and wait for God to know us.

When you feel utterly exhausted from fighting your thoughts, say to yourself: "It is futile to contend with them any longer," and then fall down before them like a captive or coward. For in doing this you commend yourself to God in the midst of your enemies and admit the radical impotence of your nature. (*Cloud*, 88–89)

This complete release, this ultimate letting go, catapults us into a space that appears to be completely empty.

But . . . you say: "Where then shall I be? By your reckoning I am to be nowhere!" Exactly. In fact, you have expressed it rather well, for I would indeed have you be nowhere. Why? Because nowhere, physically, is everywhere spiritually. (*Cloud*, 136)

We are no longer in control. All our understanding about God is suddenly of no use to us. In fact, our understanding about anything of the world is suddenly like sinking sand (see Matt. 7:26-27). Even our desire for God no longer serves us, for silent contemplation requires that we go beyond even our positive, spiritual desires. As Saint John of the Cross tells us, the soul cannot

pass to this high estate of union with God if first it void not the desire of all things, natural and supernatural . . . ; for there is the greatest possible distance between these things and that which comes to pass in this estate [union], which is naught else than transformation in God. (*Ascent of Mount Carmel*, 29)

PRACTICING APOPHATIC PRAYER

How do you practice this unknowing? The method itself is disarmingly simple.

If you want to gather all your desire into one simple word that the mind can easily retain, choose a short word. . . . A one-syllable word such as "God" or "love" is best. . . . Then fix it in your mind so that it will remain there come what may. (*Cloud*, 56)

You pick a simple holy word that captures your desire to know God; perhaps choose that word for yourself right now. Then you bring it to your attention and focus your desire for God upon that word. Each time your mind wanders, bring your attention back to this word. Unlike the Jesus Prayer, this word is not to be repeated over and over. Rather the word serves as a focal point to which you can return your attention whenever you have strayed into the land of thought. That is all.

THE CHALLENGES OF APOPHATIC PRAYER

Now some books on apophatic prayer will tell you all about its wonderful virtues—how peaceful it is, how you will experience the fullness of God in your soul, how your mind will become quiet and restful in the lap of your Creator. Unfortunately these books are guilty of the sin of omission. They leave out a few things.

I remember quite clearly the dismayed look on the face of a man who came to my wife and me to talk about contemplative prayer. We were living at a monastery whose ministry was silent prayer, and this man had come to the community for a retreat. He had read about the wonders of silent contemplative prayer and was looking forward to a fantastic experience with God. What he had encountered was just the opposite.

He told us he couldn't stop thinking, and his mind was racing twenty-four hours a day. He couldn't even sleep peacefully. The periods of silent prayer in chapel were a living nightmare, and he felt like a complete idiot because somehow he wasn't doing something right. Then to top it all off, when he was coming down the stairs that morning, he slipped and landed flat on his back on the landing.

"As I lay there," he said, "I thought, *This is wonderful. I am going to die right here, killed by a meditation retreat.*"

I had to laugh. Not at the man's pain but because what he had encountered came closer to the reality of our experience with apophatic prayer than the flowery descriptions he had read in books. Now this is not to say that we cannot have a wonderful experience with silent contemplation. We can; and the more we practice, the more we will. However, the first thing most of us encounter in silent prayer is the fallen reality of our own minds; and this experience can be painful.

When we enter into the world of no images, our mind attempts to fill this space with something. In many ways this effort is the essence of sin: We do not wait for God; rather we zoom off on our own, trying to be the master of our self and of the world. So in silent contemplative prayer, rather than wait for God's grace to give us the gift of God's presence, we fill the empty space of our mind with our own thoughts, feelings, ideas, and projects.

One of the most prominent thoughts occurring to good Christians who, unfortunately, tend to be judgmental and self-critical, is that we are doing something wrong. This thought often triggers intense feelings of anger and rejection. At one silent prayer retreat, I was amazed that no matter often we, the leaders, told participants they couldn't do the practice incorrectly, they continued to feel they were making a mistake because they couldn't quiet their minds.

In apophatic prayer we encounter ourselves. We encounter our own self-loathing, our own self-hatred; we encounter our feelings of shame and our lack of self-worth. The English writer of *The Cloud of Unknowing* says that this experience can be "as terrible as a glimpse of hell" (*Cloud*, 137). We see how little control we really have. These realities are painful, and one response is to project them onto others. So the retreat leaders suddenly become worthless. Or they are not really Christians, or they are judging the retreatants, secretly thinking bad thoughts behind their backs.

At this moment we are lost within the cloud of unknowing. This is where we must admit that we are helpless before God. We must trust our Creator to come and find us. As we return to our sacred word, over and over, that syllable in the depth of our being becomes like a sonar ping moving out into the darkness while we await the echo return. The word symbolizes our cry, "I am here, God," to which eventually comes the soft reply, "You are mine and you are loved."

One thing you must realize about the practice of apophatic prayer is that you cannot quiet your mind. Don't even try. Give up; it is a hopeless cause. There is nothing to do but wait within the nothingness of the prayer's external silence. And then something happens; "finally there will come a moment when he [the one praying] experiences such peace and repose in that darkness that he thinks surely it must be God himself" (*Cloud*, 138). God shows up. Not because of anything you have done. Not because of your own efforts. Not because you have figured it out or done it right but because God's promises are true and because God seeks you out and desires to transform your heart and mind into the likeness of Christ.

These moments of grace challenge us as much as moments of pain and suffering. Why? Two reasons. First, they cause us to feel we have achieved something. We think, *I have arrived at that farther shore. I have found God. I have conquered my sin.* Notice the construction of these sentences: They revolve around "I." "I" have done something. We take a gift from God and turn it into a possession, an accomplishment. Suddenly God is no longer in the picture. We may even stop praying at this point: *Well, I've got that one down; now on to the next chapter.* Yet as soon as we assume that attitude, we have given up praying; we have achieved nothing. Our visions of grandeur are another illusion, as dangerous as the visions of hell that preceded them. Our ancient writer admonishes, "Learn to forget not only every creature and its deeds, but yourself as well, along with whatever you may have accomplished in God's service" (*Cloud*, 102).

The second reason these feelings of peace and union with God can challenge us is that they vanish almost as quickly as they came. Suddenly we are cast back into the abyss. We no longer feel wonderful and close to God. We return to the sense of being lost; only this time the feeling may be intensified because we now know the glory of what we are missing.

The appropriate response to either of these reactions is simply to return to our word. We neither cling to a positive experience of God nor reject a negative experience of our own mind. For both of these experiences come to us from the world of images and thoughts, and this practice of apophatic prayer encourages us to move continually beyond any thought into the silence of God. Whatever arises, we go back to our word.

At this point you may be wondering, *What is the point of this prayer?* You do nothing, you know nothing, and you disregard even positive experiences! In fact, I was once asked at a retreat, "What is the purpose of silent prayer?" To which I replied, "There is no purpose." From our perspective as people who are always trying to achieve something, there is no purpose to this practice. The point is simply to place ourselves at the mercy of God and allow ourselves to be filled with the grace of our Creator. *But surely*, you insist, *there must be some fruits; there must be something that happens with this practice!* This brings me to a discussion of silent prayer in groups.

Apophatic Prayer in Groups

Although it is a solitary practice, apophatic prayer is best done with a group of people. For one reason, it is a hard practice, and the group members lend support to one another, even in the silence. Second, the fruits of the prayer become most apparent within a community.

Like the prayer, the group technique is simple. Everyone sits together to do the practice. It is often easiest for people to close their eyes, but if that is not comfortable, individuals may hold their gaze downward, focused on a point on the floor six to eight feet in front of them. Good posture is important: back straight, hands in the lap. Some people are comfortable sitting on pillows on the floor.

A leader starts the prayer and ends the prayer at the appointed time. Continuing the prayer for the allotted time period is important, somewhere between twenty and forty-five minutes. I prefer the longer time period. If you are doing the practice on a retreat and wish to pray for a still longer block of time, perhaps a few hours, then it would be advisable to alternate some time walking with times of sitting. During the time of walking, everyone continues doing the prayer (obviously with eyes open!).

The leader can begin the prayer time by saying, "Let us pray," and end the prayer period with "Amen." Some people like to say the Lord's Prayer at the end of the prayer time. Another option is to ring a bell to begin and end the prayer time, for throughout history Christians have been called to prayer by the community chimes.

What happens when a group does silent contemplative prayer together over a period of time is quite miraculous. First people begin to "soften." Although we cannot force it to happen, over time our minds do relax. They begin to slow down, and our thoughts torment us less. Along with this change comes a transformation in our physical features, a shift that becomes especially obvious during a retreat. When an outsider comes into a silent prayer retreat, the person often comments on how "soft" everyone looks. The hard edges we set to get through the world begin to rub away. Our faces relax along with our minds; shoulders begin to sink down; hearts begin to open up. The love of God starts to shine in our eyes.

As these changes take place, another phenomenon occurs: People begin to truly love each other. Even though we never speak to anyone during the time of prayer, we find ourselves feeling tremendous compassion for the other people in the room. We begin to care about our brothers and sisters in a new way. If we practice prayer regularly with a church group, as time goes on we want to listen to the others in the group more and talk less. We suddenly desire to reach out to those we don't know too well, those whom we thought we didn't like. In this way, the fruits of the prayer gradually begin to ripen in the community; as we allow God to form us, the effects of the prayer become manifest.

A group can also be useful for debriefing the experiences of apophatic prayer. However, a word of caution is in order here. Just as one should not dwell on one's thoughts during the prayer, the group discussion is not an arena for analyzing anyone's prayer experience or for comparing expectations or "results" of the prayer. The group simply listens to one another and offers support as each member struggles to be faithful to the practice. In the end, each member of the group can encourage the others simply to go back to their word.

The community practice of apophatic prayer is in itself another paradox. For although this prayer is the most radical encounter with silence and solitude of any practice in our faith, it was meant to be done in community! This is because the result of the prayer is the manifestation of the kingdom of God. For as the one God starts to shine through each person praying, we begin to see Jesus in one another. We experience the love of God, the love of self, and the love of neighbor—the three elements necessary for a spiritual life.

Now go back to your word.

FIVE

THE EXAMEN
God in Day-to-Day Life

TRAVELING COMPANION
Saint Ignatius

*Whereas silent prayer seeks to move us
beyond this world of ours, the examen assists us
in finding the God who is moving toward us,
who is reaching into our world to save us.*

he year was 1521. A "dapper young Spanish courtier" named Iñigo de Loyola had been wounded in battle, and as he "lay in bed, his thoughts alternated between the prospect of worldly glory and the following of Christ" (*Spiritual Exercises*, xiv). What should he do?

We have all experienced such times of uncertainty and doubt. Which way should the path of our lives lead? How is God calling us? Did Jesus take a left or a right at the fork in the road? When Ignatius of Loyola faced his moment of indecision, in a gift of sheer grace, he made a stunning realization. Surveying his options, Ignatius noticed that "the secular romances left a certain dryness and restlessness in their wake, whereas the sacred scenarios left him peaceful and contented" (*Spiritual Exercises,* xiv–xv). The latter set of feelings, Ignatius observed, were similar to the fruits of the Spirit (Gal. 5:22-23), whereas the former were not. As he watched these contrasting feelings arise, Ignatius recognized that God had designed his being such that it gave him hints as to which choice was from God and which was not. This understanding formed the core of Ignatius's masterful work *The Spiritual Exercises*, one of Christianity's most famous texts. In this chapter we will explore the spiritual practice of examining our daily lives for signs of God's presence.

We come to this practice from the mists of the cloud of unknowing. Both silent prayer and the Jesus Prayer took us into the world of the transcendent God, the God who is bigger than all we can imagine and whose brilliance burns away all that we can even think about the One who has no name. But most of us will not spend our days caught up in blissful union with God. We live in the

NOTE: The appendix offers step-by-step instructions for practicing the examen individually or with a group.

nitty-gritty of the world. We go to work, spend time with our friends, wash dishes, and do chores. Isn't there a prayer practice for these times?

Saint Ignatius's prayer of examination (or the examen, as it has come to be called) is a prayer practice that seeks the immanent—meaning close-by, near, or indwelling—aspect of God. This is the God who is with us always. This is the God who knows our thoughts before we think them. It is the God who is in everything and is at the heart of all. Yet even in this nearness God remains hidden, and so we need a method of prayer that brings the light of God clearly into focus; this is the point of the examen.

MAKING SENSE OF THE WORLD

To understand this practice, let us first look at the nature of our experience. In the song "Love Is the Seventh Wave," the musician Sting describes the nature of our reality as an "Empire of the senses," a place within which each of us is "queen." Here he captures in lyrics the truth that most of the time we live in a unique world of our own creation.

At every moment millions of bits of sensory data bombard us, and with them we make sense of the world around us. We organize these data in a coherent manner, and the pattern of this organization depends on our personal habits and dispositions. One person sees a sunset and appreciates beauty; another curses the sunset because it is getting dark too early. The sunset is the same, and yet the two observers—the two "queens," to use Sting's word—interpret it differently.

The power of this process is so great that we are not even aware of it, and most of the time we wander lost in our own world. The examen seeks to answer the question

Where is God in all this? Whereas silent prayer seeks to move us beyond this world of ours, the examen helps us find the God who is moving toward us, who is reaching into our world to save us.

Jesus is always trying to get our attention, but where is he? Is he in the beauty of the sunset, or is he trying to comfort us in our sadness at the coming of darkness? Ignatius responds to that question by declaring it all but impossible to answer in the present moment! Unless very practiced in the life of prayer, one finds determining whether or not an experience is of God extraordinarily difficult. This conclusion comes out of a basic assumption of the examen, that two types of "spirits" exist in the world. The solution to this problem lies in using one of the basic properties of our reality: time. Let me explain.

MOVING TOWARD OR AWAY FROM GOD

A traditional Christian view of the universe lies at the heart of the examen: Good and evil are both at work in the world, carried out by good and evil spirits. The good spirits are from God, and they try to influence us toward a life of godliness. The evil spirits are at the disposal of Satan, and they are trying to lead us into a life of sin and depravity.

Today not all people necessarily share this view of the world. Many contemporary people believe there is no such thing as evil and no such thing as objective right and wrong. If you hold these views, understanding the examen may be hard. However, even individuals who do not believe in a personified evil spirit—the devil—still seem to believe people have the capacity to become more "holy," "spiritual," or some other equivalent term. So even though acknowledging a negative spiritual direction or force may be difficult, people may understand that we can move in a positive spiritual direction. Often they translate this belief into the language of ethics; for example, being kind to others is better than being mean to them.

Whatever language you use to understand or express such concepts about reality, it is important to realize that at the core of the examen is the notion that individuals engage in actions that move them either toward or away from God. However—and this difficulty lies at the heart of finding God in the present—movement in either direction can appear "good" in the present moment. In modern-day language we use the word *denial* to describe being involved in activities that are bad for us while convincing ourselves that these behaviors are not a problem. The addict may think that getting drunk every day is a fine thing. Although everyone around this person can see that the drinking is not "of God," the one drinking is blind to his or her own sin. We can rationalize stealing from or cheating our neighbor; we can, at times, even see killing as a good thing.

If either spirit can appear to be from God in the present moment, then what is the solution for the person who wishes to follow God? Ignatius bases his answer to this question on Paul's understanding that the movement of spirits bears fruit (Gal. 5:22-23). Thus he used the reality of time to help him find the working of God in his life.

To find God in the present, Ignatius begins by looking at the past: How did his thoughts and feelings unfold over time? What were the results of his desires and actions? Ignatius sees that although in the mind of the beginner the evil spirits can hide in the moment, they cannot conceal their purposes forever. At some point they reveal that they are leading a person in a direction away from God; "the course of thoughts suggested to us may terminate in something evil. . . . These things are a clear sign that the thoughts are proceeding from the evil spirit" (*Spiritual Exercises*, 120). Continuing with the example of the addict: Although for a while the person may be able to think that getting drunk is good, by the time he or she has lost family, job, and house, hiding the evil in that course of action is impossible.

By using the vehicle of time, looking back at his experience, Ignatius is able to review any part of his life and notice whether this review gives him a sense of "consolation" or "desolation."

> I call it consolation when an interior movement is aroused in the soul, by which it is inflamed with love of its Creator and Lord. . . .
>
> I call desolation . . . darkness of soul, turmoil of spirit, . . . inclination . . . from . . . temptations which lead to want of faith, want of hope, want of love. . . . For just as consolation is the opposite of desolation, so the thoughts that spring from consolation are the opposite of those that spring from desolation. (*Spiritual Exercises*, 115–16)

Just as an airplane leaves a vapor trail in the sky, Ignatius realizes that God leaves a trail of experience in our lives. The key to finding the path God leaves through our empire is to search for the evidence of that trail of experience. This search is the practice of the examen.

PRACTICING THE EXAMEN

Like most of our prayer techniques, this one is fairly simple. We begin by preparing ourselves to listen for God. Ignatius feels two steps are required for such preparation.

The first step is *proper intention,* achieved by calling to mind the purpose for your existence: "I must consider only the end for which I am created, that is, for the praise of God our Lord and for the salvation of my soul" (*Spiritual Exercises,* 55). Reminding yourself of this purpose helps prevent distraction by desires centered only on yourself or away from God; it reminds you that you are seeking only that which is God's will and God's presence in your life.

The second step is a direct extension of the first. If you are created only for the work of God, then you need to arrive at *a state of "indifference to all created things. . . .* [That is,] as far as we are concerned, we should not prefer health to sickness, riches to poverty, honor to dishonor, a long life to a short life" (*Spiritual Exercises,* 12; italics added). This means that as much as possible, you need to begin your prayer without prejudice. Just because you "like" something does not mean that it is from God. Similarly you may find God most active in intensely unpleasant experiences. In order to see God's actions in your life, you need to be open to possibilities that go beyond obvious choices or desires. To do this you must arrive at a place of interior indifference. As Mary the mother of Jesus said, "Let it be with me according to your word" (Luke 1:38).

Once you arrive at this state of clear intention and indifference (at least to the best of your ability), reflect on the chosen period of time. This could be a day, a week, an hour. It can be a general period of time or a single experience, such as a youth-group meeting or a worship service. Whatever the chosen period, take a while to review the whole experience. What were your feelings during that time? What are your thoughts now? Notice how your body felt. Ignatius realized the importance of using all our faculties as we seek God: "All the powers of the individual are to be engaged—the intellect, the memory, the imagination, the heart, the will, and the senses" (*Spiritual Exercises*, xx). Bring your powers of awareness and attention to these observations:

- Which are the feelings of life and love that stir in you a movement toward God?
- What thoughts or memories leave you feeling dry, dead, stale and thus move you away from the vitality of a living Creator?
- Ignatius tells us to "carefully observe the whole course of our thoughts" (*Spiritual Exercises,* 119). Do your thoughts begin with feelings of light and love but end with emptiness?
- Do you continue to desire and love God even if you are struggling with something painful?

As you perform this reflection, you may begin to see patterns of consolation and desolation emerging. These patterns represent the flow of good and evil spirits Ignatius described. At first they may be hard to see clearly; however, as time goes on, you will develop a sense of which experiences are "of God" and which are not.

THE PRACTICE IN ACTION

It was a dark time in my life. My marriage was in bad shape, and although I enjoyed my graduate-school program, I wasn't sure in what direction I was headed. To say that I felt lost and confused probably is a gross understatement. In the midst of this I had made a decision to go to Nova Scotia for the summer to help build a monastery. It seemed like the perfect activity for my lost state of being.

The trouble was, I had to get there from my home in Colorado in an ancient Toyota that I usually feared driving more than the eight miles from home to school. But since getting to the monastery site by plane or other means was impractical, I decided to drive. Thus began one of the most challenging journeys of my life.

In Nebraska the transmission of the car blew up. I had decided in advance that I would pay for one major repair of the car, and so I replaced the transmission with a used one. After several more minor problems, the generator and the alternator broke in the middle of nowhere in northern Michigan. The man who picked me up on the side of the road owned a junkyard and I decided, after some calling and research, to give him the car and get a ride to the nearest bus station, one hundred miles away. Because I now needed to travel light, I gave away most of the stuff in the car, including my treasured toolbox.

After reaching Toronto, I was to take a train to northern Nova Scotia where someone from the monastery would pick me up. I arrived in Toronto at about 8:00 in the evening, and my train wasn't leaving until 6:00 the next morning. I decided to look around the city for a while and then spend the night in the train station. However when I got to the train station at about 11:00, I found it locked; and when I returned to the bus station, it too was shut for the night. I spent the entire night wandering around down-town Toronto.

Now what about the examen? Although I had not yet become a Christian, I had learned the practice of the exa-men. So at every step of my bizarre and horrific journey, I would look back at my decisions along the way: the deci-sion to go to the monastery in the first place, the decision to give away my car and all my possessions, the decision to keep going even as the cost of the trip mounted; and, I was stranded in one place after another. Believe it or not, as crazy and impossible as it seems, every examination produced the same result: consolation—keep going.

I did make it to that monastery, and a year and a half later at that same place I had a powerful conversion experience and came to know Jesus. If I had never gone there, who knows how different my life might have been? The examen helped me to continue when all "worldly" logic would have said give up, go home.

THE EXAMEN IN GROUPS

What about group situations? God does not work only in and through the lives of individuals, and the examen offers an excellent practice for coming to understand God's active presence in our collective life. The examen can be practiced in a group in two general ways: (1) by sharing individual reflections, and (2) by applying the examen to a common group activity.

The first group approach resembles other group methods discussed earlier. When the group gathers, members take time in silence for each person to reflect back upon a particular time period. Then each member takes a turn sharing his or her personal reflections. I use this technique with my youth-group religious education classes. The students take some time to reflect on places where God has been active in their lives since our last meeting. The whole process allows the group to get to know one another, share in our spiritual lives together, and come to understand more about how God can work in varied ways with different people. In this method, the members of the group may comment on some of the sharings, but usually these comments are kept to a minimum.

The second method for a group application of the examen is the prayerful reflection upon a group activity. This use of the practice can be quite exciting and a valuable way for a group to grow together in living out God's will. The group reflects on an activity common to the group and then shares their individual reflections upon the group event. The common activity can be anything: a youth event, a worship service, a job or service project, or a church board meeting. During a time of quiet, each member of the group performs the examen on the designated activity. Following the silent time, the group members share their observations.

What begins to unfold during the sharing time is a rich and deep reflection on how God is moving in the group—this is the process of *discernment*—a fancy word that just means searching for the will or presence of God in a given situation. Because several different people are examining the common activity, the group can see multiple perspectives on how God is or is not acting during the time together.

NEW DIRECTIONS FOR MINISTRY

At the church I currently serve, the worship team and the various Christian education programs practice this group examen for our respective activities. What never ceases to impress me about this prayer time is the richness of our collective reflections. When looking back on worship, one person may have appreciated the music, while another felt a consolation in the prayer time, and a third felt God's presence through the look on a child's face. Through this practice, we see the multiple ways that God works in a given situation, and this backward glance allows us to begin to see God in present and future situations as well.

As we pray, God begins to suggest directions for our ministry that bring new life and energy to all that we do. For example, at the end of each school year, the Sunday school teachers and I go on retreat, during which we practice the examen. We pray about the year and how God is present or not present in our Sunday school classes. One year it became very clear that the teachers felt a lack of God's presence when they were inadequately prepared for what they were teaching. As a result of this realization, we revamped our class schedule to provide teachers additional training time every month. The benefits of this change were impressive. The teachers' confidence improved, as did their ability to transmit the faith to their students. The prayer helped to show us where God was leading so that the Spirit could become more present in our midst.

Such change was Ignatius's original purpose as he lay in bed contemplating his life, trying to make a decision about the future. The ultimate application of the examen reveals how God has or has not worked in the past, enabling us to more clearly follow God's will in the present and on into the future. Ignatius writes that one way to make a good choice in life is "when much light and understanding are derived through experience of desolations and consolations" (*Spiritual Exercises*, 57). Thus as we come to understand how God is working in our lives through the use of the examen, we can also see the choices and directions in which God would lead us—choices that move us toward consolation and away from desolation. As we become increasingly indifferent to anything other than what God would have us do and diligently seek God's will and movement in our lives, we can experience the presence of God in the moment. It is this experience of God in the present that leads us to action in tune with our Maker.

"The love that moves and causes one to choose must descend from above, that is, from the love of God" (*Spiritual Exercises*, 59). Experiencing this love through the examination of spirits naturally draws us to it. When our worship team practices the examen on our worship service and witnesses the powerful presence of God in our midst, we are drawn to create new services that will allow that presence to shine forth. Thus the examen of the past pulls us like a magnet into the open arms of a loving God who becomes more and more real to us in our endless string of present moments.

SIX

CREATIVITY AND THE DIVINE
To Create Is to Pray

TRAVELING COMPANION
Hildegard of Bingen

*Since prayer connects us to God,
creativity—as it connects us
to the creative power of God—
becomes a prayer practice.*

he trajectory of our prayer practices is slowly and inevitably drawing us out into the world around us; from the silent, solitary reflection upon scripture to the dark cloud of unknowing to the gentle resonance of the name of Jesus, we are led into an examination of the traces of God in our lives. This is the nature of a life with God: Our experiences of the Holy naturally lead beyond ourselves, as God seeks to use us to show the power of divine love to others.

What happens now? What happens as our hearts begin to beat with that slow steady pulse of the heart of the Trinity? We yearn to create. As we turn in prayer to God, the great Creator who made heaven and earth, we become vessels of creative energy and desire. We long to give expression to the gift we have received, and as we do so, the act of creation becomes a prayer in itself, a way to seek union with the One who sustains our very being.

In this chapter we will meet an extraordinary woman who used creative expression to give life to her visions of God. We shall learn that for Hildegard of Bingen, creativity not only was a means for *expressing* her prayer but was itself prayer. In her revelation of the divine, Hildegard came to know that creative expression is part of the fullness of the presence of God.

> For after we have received the life-giving spirit in our mother's womb, once we have been born in this way and begun to express ourselves in action, our own worth is apparent in the terms of the works which the soul performs with the body. (*Mystical Writings*, 71–73)

NOTE: The appendix offers step-by-step instructions for practicing creative prayer individually or with a group.

Hildegard was born in 1098 in what we now know as Germany. At an early age her parents gave her to a convent. She died at age eighty-one, in 1179, in the convent she had founded. At the age of three she received the first of a series of powerful divine visions. For a long time she hesitated to share these with anyone, but eventually others encouraged her to bring forth the gifts God had given her.

Despite spending much of her life ill in bed, Hildegard exerted significant influence upon the church in Europe. Not only did she become a strong voice in church reform, advising popes and other church leaders, but she was also a poet, visual artist, musician, healer, and gardener. Truly it seemed that the creative power of God, a power that Hildegard described as "greening power," flowed from her in a raging torrent (*Mystical Writings*, 32).

THE NATURE OF CREATIVITY

What is creativity and how, really, is it connected to prayer and God? If the notion of creativity as a prayer practice is to make any sense, we must try to answer this challenging question (almost as hard as the question, What is art?).

Let's begin with the Bible. The scriptures present God's ability to create the world out of nothing as a fundamental characteristic of God. We read about it first in the opening passages of Genesis (Gen. 1:1) and see this aspect of God lifted up again and again throughout our sacred texts. God forms people and animals (for example, Gen. 1:20-27; Ps. 139:13); God brings forth beings (Ps. 104:24) and justice (Isa. 33:5); God sets up the foundations of the world with Wisdom at the side of the Creator (Prov. 8:28-30).

Creativity is the sign that God is God; no one else can create as God creates. In Hildegard's words,

The Spirit of God is a life that bestows life. . . .
She is glistening life . . .
all-awakening,
all resurrecting. (*Hildegard*, 69)

Furthermore, this creativity connects to another one of God's essential attributes, love. It is God's love that calls forth the creatures God creates. Hildegard's vision of the fountain of life, the fountain from which creation springs, captures this essential connection:

God embraces in his great love all things whose reflection appeared in the leaping fountain before he ordered them to come forth in their own shape. And in me, Love, all things are reflected and my splendour reveals the design of things. (*Mystical Writings*, 101)

Hildegard sees that human beings, created by God, are "rooted in [God and Love] like a reflected image, just as the semblance of each thing is seen in the water [of the fountain of life]" (*Mystical Writings*, 99–101). In the creative process, according to Hildegard, God creates people, who are themselves born and fashioned to create as the life and love of God flows through them. So, just as God sees visions of what is to be created and then creates, so too we are designed to see visions and create in accordance with the power and presence of God in our lives. "Humanity too is God's creation. But humanity alone is called to co-operate with God in the creation" (*Mystical Writings*, 28).

At one point in the movie *Pollock,* a biography of the artist Jackson Pollock, the artist receives a commission for his first huge painting. It is a canvas the size of an entire wall in a fairly large room. For days, Jackson sits in the room doing nothing. He paces, he sits in the corner, his eyes bore holes in the canvas. The deadline for the painting's delivery draws closer, and still he has not even picked up a brush. Finally he rises up off the floor to approach the canvas. He picks up a huge brush and begins. Within a few hours the painting is done.

What Pollock was searching and waiting for was his vision. Once this had appeared, he needed only to render the vision on the canvas. Perhaps you know artists who talk about seeing things in their head or hearing songs; they are called to create out of nothing, just as God created out of nothing. Since prayer connects us to God, creativity—as it connects us to the creative power of God—becomes a prayer practice.

OBSTACLES TO CREATIVITY

Unfortunately one significant obstacle blocks this particular practice; perhaps you have already encountered it even in reading these few pages. Our society teaches us from an early age that most of us are not "artists." Trampling the natural impulse for creativity represents one of our culture's great manifestations of sin.

Recently I asked a group of seventh graders to write their own psalms, using a line from one of the biblical psalms as a starting point. From the outset this activity terrified them. They protested that they "couldn't do it," that they were "bad at writing," that they "didn't know what to say." It took a huge effort on my part to finally get them to relax enough to complete their psalms.

Then I wanted the group members to read the psalms aloud to everyone. This began another painful round of protests that their work was "bad," that they couldn't possibly share it. One girl was so terrified that I had to sit next to her and read with her. When we finally got all of the pieces read, they were wonderful; the problem was, the kids couldn't see the beauty in their work. At this tender age, they already had been convinced that they were incapable of creating.

Many of us are in the same position. We feel that we are "bad at art," that we can't draw or sculpt or play music or write. This feeling has been generated by comments from adults in our life who had the same ideas pounded into their heads. Together with Satan, we as a society have unconsciously conspired to cut ourselves off from the very creative power given to us by God at our birth. God wants us to use this creative power for the good of God's creation, and as we respond to this calling, our prayer life becomes a movement toward that creative force.

When we orient our lives around the practice of prayer, our sense that we lack creativity slowly melts away, and we find that we long to create. I observed this shift during a recent retreat. In one of the exercises, I asked participants to reflect upon their desires in relation to their own sense of health and spirituality. More than half the people in the group came back from the exercise talking about their desire to create. They also spoke about noticing a direct correlation between the amount of time they had for creative endeavors and their sense of health and connection to God: The less time they spent creating, the more distant God seemed in their lives. Yet even though these people had drifted away from their creative endeavors, after only a short time in prayer, they once again became aware of the desire to create. This shift in awareness occurs so quickly and easily because God has formed us as creative beings. As Hildegard says, "The rational soul is inserted in the body, as though in a vessel of clay; so that, through it, the body may be guided in its mode of living and the heavenly soul [God] may be contemplated through faith" (*Mystical Writings*, 143).

CREATIVITY AS PRAYER

So what is the practice itself? Unlike the other prayer practices I have presented so far, this practice has no set form; there are literally infinite ways to "do" creativity, because God gifts us all with unique abilities. I will simply outline here a general overview of how this practice can work, giving some examples along the way. For those of you who cannot imagine doing this practice on your own, the group setting may be particularly valuable.

We begin this practice by paying close attention to the intention and attitude we bring to our prayer. We start with the realization that we are already doing the practice! Many activities we label "work" or "chores" or "the drudgery of life" actually hold potential as creative endeavors. So an essential part of the practice is bringing your awareness and the skill of noticing into daily life. What are some of the things that you are already creating: a family; a living space, a church, a job environment, a daily schedule, schoolwork, a sports team? If you were to make a list of all the possible starting points for creative prayer, it might look something like this:

- Decorating your house or room
- Getting dressed
- Art in school or other settings
- Cooking

- Your ministry or other job
- Activities in which you and your friends participate
- Writing projects

In all of these undertakings, the "greening power" of God is present and active. Are you aware of it? Hildegard heard God saying in her vision, "By means of the airy wind, I stir everything into quickness with a certain invisible life which sustains all. For the air lives in its green power and its blossoming; the waters flow as if they were alive" (*Mystical Writings*, 91). The practice begins as you see that you are already involved in the creative process. If you are like those seventh graders who already were conditioned to say no to creativity, you must ask God to help you overcome this obstacle. Begin your time of creative prayer by asking God to give you the knowledge of your creative potential.

After you have made clear your desire to know God in creativity, the next step in this prayer practice is to start noticing what creative activities naturally draw your interest. You may be attracted to the traditional arts; building things may appeal; creating an organization or ordering some little part of the world over which you have responsibility may get you excited. Maybe you love to garden, sew, or organize social events. As you open yourself to the all-pervasive reality of the creative power of God, you begin to see creativity blossoming everywhere.

For example, a woman who is just beginning to take her faith life more seriously talked to me about writing thank-you notes to people who had expressed sympathy or been helpful at the time of her mother's death. She told me she had always dreaded this sort of task before, but on this occasion she found herself wanting to take the time to say something special and particular to each person. She found herself imagining the person she was writing to, remembering what she or he had said to her at the funeral. Then she would think of a unique message for each individual. As she did this, she found herself filled with a wonderful sense of joy and appreciation and love. Later I heard from some of the recipients about these cards and how amazing each one was. In this creative activity, the woman had connected with the power and presence of God's love; and the experience enriched not only herself but also those around her.

So seek out the activities that draw you in. Continue to notice the obstacles that arise—"this is a waste of time," "I can't draw," and other such interior self-talk—ask God to help you overcome them and give you the courage to continue your creative endeavor. Then go on with your activity.

Another possibility for creative prayer is to combine creative action with other prayer practices. For example, if you are practicing *lectio divina* and a particularly vivid image comes to you, take the time to draw the image. Don't worry if the drawing isn't perfect or even correct; let the process of drawing become a new time of prayer. What is God calling out of you in the artwork? What new realizations come to you? What new things are you learning about your relationship with God?

CREATIVITY IN GROUPS

Probably many of you are still saying, "This practice sounds way too hard to do on my own!" This brings me to practicing creativity in groups. Even for people comfortable with the practice of creativity, the group setting provides a wonderful place to deepen and enrich this prayer; for those who feel completely lost, it is a great place to begin.

The purpose of a group setting is to provide a structured time and a specific creative activity. A youth group, a prayer group, or a retreat planning committee can designate a session for creative prayer. During this session, people will get a chance to become comfortable with the practice and to experience the process of creativity, which in turn will help them to recognize creativity at other times in their lives.

The group leader or planning committee picks a creative activity for the group. Choose an exercise with both structure and flexibility and prepare accordingly. Thus if the group will use visual art materials, have a whole range of supplies available: pens, paper, clay, paints, materials to cut out for collages, glue, scissors, crayons, pastels, tape, and so on. What the members of the group do during the prayer time is limited only by the leader's imagination. Here are some possible scenarios for participants:

- Reflect on scripture and then create artwork in response to your reflections.
- Spend some time in silence asking God to show you the nature of your desire for God and then respond to that with art.
- Draw a lifeline, noting times when you particularly felt God's presence in your life.
- Pray about a specific question presented by the leader and then create something that expresses the answers arising out of your silent reflection.

It is important for leaders to trust that God is present and active for the group members. No matter what the assignment, amazing responses will be evoked.

After group members spend time on their creations, they are invited to share the results with one another. This time is valuable. As people speak aloud or show the outcome of their creative prayer, the experience is rein-forced. Recognizing in the group that this indeed has been a time of prayer increases the desire for more such times. Even in this aspect of the practice, Hildegard serves as an example. Not until she shared her visions did they become a real force both in her life and in the life of the church. As with any group practice, end your time together with a prayer of thanks to God for providing the experience.

CREATIVE WORSHIP

One special category of creative prayer with groups is wor-ship. Liturgical art is currently enjoying a great revival, a trend over which we should all rejoice. Presenting scripture and prayer through art helps people experience the power and presence of God in an extraordinary way.

As with a small group, the possibilities for creative wor-ship are endless. For a worship planning team, creating liturgical art is itself a prayer practice. As the team engages in prayerful reflection on an upcoming service, the mem-bers begin to see possibilities for artistic expression in worship. Perhaps they are drawn to do a drama about a particular scripture; maybe they wish to decorate the sanc-tuary according to the liturgical season. Maybe banners or decorations could enhance a sermon series. Or maybe the group feels drawn to audiovisual presentations or videos. The list goes on and on.

This is the beauty of the practice of creativity: It is self-sustaining and it unfolds endlessly. As we begin to understand creativity as a prayer practice, we can bring our attention to the times when we are already creative, and we can notice God in many areas of our lives. Because the Word of God continues into infinity, we become fountains of living water once we tap into that boundless source of sustained creativity.

One simple but beautiful example of creativity is decorating a backpack. A friend of mine who is in school carries her books in a daypack. On the outside of this pack she loves to put buttons, decals, and sew-on labels. Many express her faith; others are just beautiful. What began as a simple daypack has now become a living testimony to her prayer life and, through beauty, to the creative presence of God. Each time I see this piece of art, I am reminded of my own faith—it is a prayerful moment.

As we end this chapter, let us listen to the echo of Hildegard, a herald of the creative power of God:

> When my soul experiences the sight of these things [visions of God], I am transformed into another character. . . . And . . . my soul drinks as though from a spring; but the spring remains full and undepleted. But no hour is my soul without the light I spoke of, which is called "the reflection of the living light." (*Mystical Writings*, 146)

SEVEN

JOURNALING
Writing What God Shows Us

TRAVELING COMPANION
Julian of Norwich

*In the practice of journaling,
we bridge these two worlds—the world of God's Word
and the world of our words—
in an attempt to communicate
to ourselves and others that
which God would have us hear and know.*

*W*e are coming to the last of the practices I have labeled "mental" practices—those in which our mind is the primary vehicle for the encounter with God. Thus it is fitting now to explore a practice that actually has been with us from the beginning of the book, the practice of journaling or writing.

What do I mean by saying this practice "has been with us"? If the figures we have met in these pages had not been called to write about their prayer experiences, then we never would have known about them or even that these people existed. The revelations of God that entered the minds of these saints would have burned their impression upon a single creature and then vanished from sight, lost to history and to all of humanity.

But this did not happen. Rather, many of the great pray-ers of the church were somehow compelled to put down in a form that could be preserved some trace of what they had experienced. So great was this need to share (and as we shall see, it is God's desire—not just people's) that even when the mystics such as the desert mothers and fathers refused to write, someone else wrote for them.

I have already pointed out the power of words in relation to God's Word, scripture, and highlighted the power of the spoken word in relation to sharing our experiences in a group. In the practice of journaling, we bridge these two worlds—the world of God's Word and the world of our words—in an attempt to communicate to ourselves and others that which God would have us hear and know.

NOTE: The appendix offers step-by-step instructions for journaling prayer individually or with a group.

WRITING AS PRAYER

Words hold incredible power. Words crystallize into recognizable form that which is unformed and unrecognizable. A single word can communicate a powerful emotion; a series of words, a complex thought; a page of words or a short poem, the love of God. Therefore, the practice of journaling not only stands on its own as a prayer practice but also is a practice that can be combined with any of the other practices in this book.

Through journaling a person can share experiences of *lectio* or track discernments made in the examen. One can try to plumb the depths of silent prayer or write about creativity. Finally the practice of writing stands on its own as a way of encountering God because writing cultivates those two essential prayer skills: listening and noticing. As we strive to jot down our experiences of the Holy, we enter into that silence from which God speaks. We incline our ear such that a voice beyond our own may become recognizable to us and speak words we then may capture on paper (or a computer screen).

JOURNEYING WITH JULIAN

Capturing the essence of what God spoke was the chief desire of the incredible woman who will journey with us through this chapter. Julian of Norwich lived the latter part of her life in a two-room "cell," a small apartment if you will, attached to a church in Norwich, England.

On the eighth of May 1373, Julian fell ill and began an ecstatic journey (a trancelike state of mind associated with visions of God) that resulted in sixteen powerful "showings"—visions—about the nature of God. Although Julian describes herself as "a simple creature that could not letter" (*Revelation of Love*, 4), she spent the next twenty years of her life writing about and reflecting upon these visions. Eventually her writings were compiled in a book called the *Revelation of Love,* one of the great classics of the mystical tradition. In this book, Julian reveals to us amazing things about God and her experience of God, while at the same time helping us to understand the nature and value of the practice of writing. For after her visions were over, it was the act of writing and reflection that enabled her to comprehend all she had seen.

Before I discuss the actual process of writing as prayer, I need to clarify several issues if this practice is to make sense. In some ways these issues have been with us throughout the book, but their relevance increases when we come to write about our experience of God. Julian says,

> For it was by his [God's] courteous love and from his endless goodness that he wanted to show it [Julian's revelation of God's love] to everyone, for the comfort of us all. Thus God truly wants you to receive it with every joy and gladness just as if Jesus himself had shown it to you all in person. (*Revelation of Love*, 18)

When we sit down to write, one of the first thoughts that may come to mind is, *Aren't God's words already written in the Bible? How could I write anything that would be God's speech?* In Julian's words above we hear the antidote to such concerns and the answers to our questions. For in her words, we come to know two things that she saw so clearly. The first is that God is a living presence with whom we have an active relationship in the present. The second is that God desires to speak to us. Although we may already feel comfortable with the first fact, I think we are seldom fully aware of the second.

Julian discovers that "our Lord wishes that we understand" (*Revelation of Love*, 82); God longs to infuse us with the knowledge of God's love for us. Time and time again God filled Julian's heart and mind with words relating the exquisite care and all-encompassing grace with which God desires to bless us.

> I [God] am the ground of your beseeking: first it is my will that you have it, and then I make you want it: now since I make you seek, and then you do seek, how should it then be that you should not have whom you seek? (*Revelation of Love*, 79–80)

As Julian heard the words and wrote them down, the reality of their meaning was sealed in her heart.

The immediacy of God's desire to speak to us can seem impossible. *How can the God of all creation really want or even be able to speak words directly to me?* God must be far away, a distant parent or lofty ruler.

GOD COMES CLOSE

I remember a time when the incredible miracle of God's immediacy hit me with particular force. My wife and I were on a bus in India, an experience difficult for Westerners to appreciate. Often you have a person or two sitting on your lap. Usually it is hard to breathe, and comfort is not something you even think about. On this particular trip, I was smashed up against the window toward the rear of the bus. I was tired and vaguely ill, and to distract myself from the reality inside the bus, I was gazing intently out the window.

As we passed through one town, a scene unfolded before my eyes of crowds, animals, small houses crammed together, and more crowds—the usual Indian panorama. What struck me again, for the umpteenth time since our arrival in that country, was the number of people. They were everywhere, masses of people, even in this reasonably "small" city.

Just then this thought came to me—a clear beacon shining through the fog in my brain: *God knows all these people, really knows them, knows their thoughts and feelings, their desires and histories.* It seemed a staggering impossibility. Yet I knew in that moment that it was somehow true. Like Julian, I was awed at the magnitude of God's mind and God's love. Furthermore, also like Julian, it was through the words of my thoughts that I knew this amazing truth about God, and these words have been with me for years, available for me to pray over, reflect upon, and now share with you.

Yet the notion of God coming close to speak to us is not pleasant for everyone. Many would rather keep God at a distance. The words and voices we hear in our heads are not always pleasant and loving; sometimes they are punitive and harsh. Our image of God, often formed in the image of our parents or other authority figures, can be one of a judging, wrathful figure, someone who would speak words of condemnation to us. We wouldn't want that God coming too close.

These concerns bring me to another important issue in the life of prayer: the importance of trusting God and trusting that we can directly know the love and forgiveness we often talk about at church but may not have received in our lives. If we are to allow ourselves to be intimate with God, we do need to have some sense that God can be trusted. If our image of God is the sort of negative image I mentioned above, then developing this trust is not easy.

Furthermore, we may not have the sense that God really can speak to us directly, either because we have never had this experience or perhaps because we have been taught that God speaks only to special people or certified holy people. These thoughts and feelings are perfectly natural and make our historical friends especially valuable to us. Julian herself had these same doubts and uncertainties. She knew that "many times our trust is not complete" and that we can "feel quite empty" in prayer. Yet at the same time, she has also shared with us her certainty that in her visions, it was God "who showed me, without intermediary of any kind," and what God showed was beautiful and amazing (*Revelation of Love,* 79, 7).

Julian has been to the mountaintop before us, and like Moses she has brought back writings that confirm God's gracious desires for us. We can lean on her words as we seek the words that God would have for us. We can use her experience to support us during the challenges of our own experience, holding up the light of her understanding when we enter into our own dark places.

Two Methods of Journaling

There are many ways of doing writing as prayer, and part of your journey will be to find what works for you. To help you begin, let me describe two methods I have found valuable. The first is a simple journaling process, and the second is a process of having a conversation with God.

As writing falls under the general category of creativity, you may need to work through some of the obstacles I described in the previous chapter. You may feel that you are not a "writer," that you are not good at this or cannot do it. In a time of silence, ask God to help you with these concerns. Pray for release from your anxiety; ask God to help you understand that you are not writing for performance or publication but rather writing as prayer, a gentle conversation between two beings who want to know each other. Ask for awareness of God's desire to speak to you.

The first practice is a form of basic journaling; however, the focus is not merely on events of the day but on one's relationship with God. You may want to get a special book of blank paper to write by hand, or you may feel more comfortable writing on the computer. Begin the practice by telling God of your intention to listen for God's voice in your life. Then simply start writing your thoughts and feelings in relation to the divine; you might do this every day, once a week, or whenever you notice the desire to go to your journal.

Initially you might write about the results of other prayer practices such as *lectio* or the examen. You could note the random thoughts that come into your mind as you go through your day. You may want to write the desires of your heart or your unanswered questions. Maybe you'll write that you don't know what to write! This is a conversation that God will lead, so where you start doesn't matter.

The next phase is listening. Wait for some replies. You might listen during the time you set aside for writing, or perhaps you listen as you go about your day. What is important here is not to second-guess what God might say to you or how God's reply might be perceived. Maybe it just feels like more of your own words. Maybe it is more questions, or perhaps it is the sound of sheer silence. Whatever the replies or lack thereof, write those down the next time you come to your journal. The only important thing is to begin the conversation and have faith that a conversation is actually taking place! Remember to remind God and yourself occasionally of your intention to listen for God and engage in a conversation with your Maker.

If you have never done something like this, journaling may seem silly, and you may feel that it is not working at all in the beginning. Have patience and continue to practice. Remember, Julian spent twenty years writing her one book! Over time you will begin to notice that you have a partner in your conversation. Another voice is there, and it is not your own. Jesus is indeed right there with you, communicating in the fullness of the Spirit.

If you find this open-ended journaling too vague, you may find the second method of written prayer more compelling. This technique provides a specific format for a conversation with God. Draw a line down the center of a piece of paper. The column on the left will hold your thoughts and comments; the column on the right will hold God's. You are the scribe for both. Begin the conversation with a thought, a question, a desire, or a reflection that you want to bring to God. Write this down in your column. Then listen for God's reply and write it down in God's column.

I have done this practice with many people in a variety of settings, and so I smile as I write this, knowing the look that might be on your face right now. This practice seems crazy. How could you actually write what God is saying? Is this some New Age channeling trick? Just try the practice. For every funny look I have been given at the beginning of the prayer time, I have received an equally amazed look when a person returns from the period of prayer with a conversation written on her or his paper. Yet if we take Julian seriously, we should not be surprised. God wants to talk to us! Sometimes God has a lot to say, sometimes just a few words. However, it is remarkable how this practice works.

As people write with an attitude of listening and silence coupled with an intention directed toward God, they hear replies that seem to come from beyond themselves. Julian describes being guided in the conversation: "Then our Lord took my mind back to the longing I had for him before" (*Revelation of Love*, 54). As we place ourselves at God's disposal, we are able to hear what God wants to tell us.

THE VALUE OF GROUP JOURNALING

"But how do we know it is God speaking?" some of you are, I hope, crying out. This critical question points to the value of journaling with a group and touches again on the issue of discernment.

A youth leader told me a story about starting some prayer practices with his group. The kids loved these times of prayer, and everything seemed to be going well. Then at one group session, a boy announced that he had experienced a wonderful prayer time during which God had told him it was perfectly all right to have sex with as many girls as he wanted. The group leader, fairly new to the disciplines of prayer, almost dropped dead on the spot.

We need to remember that our minds are tricky and that we possess an almost infinite capacity to deceive ourselves. Yes, God shows up and talks to us, but we also mumble to no one in particular, lost in our own world like Gollum, the creature from *The Hobbit* who went mad in the darkness of his cave. The young man in the youth group was hearing not God's voice but his own.

The value of a group for the practice of writing is in getting feedback. When we hear our own voice spoken aloud, we can listen to ourselves again and see if we are making any sense. As with the examen, we must apply the rules of good discernment to our practice of conversing with God. If our writing leads us in the direction of peace, love of self and neighbor, righteousness and goodness, then our confidence that we are engaging in genuine prayer grows. If our conversation leads in the direction of self-centeredness and away from the fruits of the Spirit, however, we need a reality check and assistance in reorienting ourselves.

A group can offer such guidance to its members. So in a group setting, you could set aside time for a conversation-with-God exercise followed by a time to reflect together and share the written conversations. Although normally feedback during the sharing is limited (remember we are not in the business of trying to fix or analyze one another's prayer time), if a major issue emerges, such as the one in the story above, the group leader might either take the opportunity to offer some group instruction or plan to schedule private time with a particular person.

WALL OF PRAYER

Before I leave the discussion of creativity, I do want to describe one group practice that can combine both the visual creative arts and the practice of writing. For the wall of prayer, the group needs a large sheet of paper such as a long piece of butcher paper or something similar. A variety of visual art supplies—pens, markers, paints, crayons, and so forth—will be used.

The group gathers around the paper to draw, write, and doodle on a particular topic, issue, or question. Reflect on scripture, respond to a question about your church, or share insights on a topic of mutual interest. After working in one spot on the paper for a while, group members rotate to another position. After several rotations, a wonderful portrait of the group's prayer has appeared. The wall of prayer can be displayed and used as an object for further group reflection and discussion.

As I close these chapters about "mental practices," I hope you are beginning to appreciate the vast space that is your mind. Also I hope you are coming to know that God longs to fill that space with the glory of God's love. Prayer initiates this process of transformation, and God fulfills it. In the words spoken by God and written by Julian:

I am the sovereign goodness of all manner of things.
I am that makes you to love.
I am that makes you to long.
I it am: the endless fulfilling of all true desires.
(*Revelation of Love*, 131–32)

EIGHT

BODY PRAYER
The Body and the Spiritual Life

TRAVELING COMPANIONS
Song of Solomon & Abelard and Heloise

God did not make us disembodied spirits. We do not float around in the ether communing with one another via telepathic thoughts. We are formed and made in material bodies that come from the dust of the earth.

I am my beloved's, and his desire is for me. Come, my
beloved, let us go forth into the fields, . . . let us go out
early to the vineyards. . . . There I will give you my love.

—SONG OF SOLOMON 7:10-12

*M*y guess is that most of us are comfortable
with the idea of holy people practicing silent
prayer in a cave by themselves. This image is a familiar
one, recognizable, and even soothing.

On the other hand, we do not easily recognize the
activity of two lovers out in the fields as contemplative
prayer. In fact, associating these two activities, making love
and contemplative prayer, might even be seen by most
Christians as the height of heresy. Yet there it is, right in
the Bible. The Song of Solomon, recognized for centuries
as a discourse on the ecstatic union with God (the state of
mind we experience when our minds are fully connected
with Christ's mind), uses the image of lovers to describe
this spiritual experience.

In this chapter we leave the primarily mental prayer
practices and begin to venture into the material world. This
process of moving outward will continue through the next
five chapters, in which I will present prayer practices that
involve our whole being and our relationships to the world
around us: to nature, to our lifestyle, to one another as we
exist in community. These chapters follow those on mental
practices for a reason: The practices described are harder to
do and require the preparation of the earlier practices.

NOTE: The appendix offers step-by-step instructions for practicing body
prayers individually or with a group.

Perhaps that last statement surprises you because the prayer activities in the previous chapters were unfamiliar, maybe even completely foreign. You might say, "I always walk in nature, I always breathe. That stuff will be easy compared to chanting a single phrase over and over or writing down God's thoughts." Yet this is exactly the problem: When we approach familiar activities, we tend to do them as we have always done them. We walk, breathe, eat, work, look at the sky all the time, and normally we don't give these activities a second thought. We certainly don't bring to them an attitude of contemplative prayer and reflection.

It is easy to see a hermit as the image of someone living a life with God; she is performing an esoteric practice that we think of as prayer. The challenge that lies before us in these next five chapters is to bring to our everyday activities the posture of the seated monk.

NEGATIVE ATTITUDES TOWARD THE BODY

I begin this phase of our journey with one of the most difficult and controversial subjects in our faith: the body, our bodies. Why is this subject so difficult? Because for centuries the church has taken the position that the body is the seat of all evil. We have rejected, marginalized, even mutilated our bodies for the sake of our faith, and the collected historical weight of this rejection has lodged in our consciousness as a vague underlying sense of shame and humiliation about our incarnated (the fact that we have bodies) beings.

I feel that it is necessary to bring up this dilemma right at the start because otherwise, anything I say about body prayer will be haunted by the shadow of negativity toward our bodies. If any of you doubt that we harbor these feelings of hatred toward our bodies, I encourage you to look on TV or in the newspaper at the thousands of ads focused on products that will change our bodies, improve our bodies, distort our bodies. Or look at the billions of dollars spent on diets, plastic surgery, or medical care for eating disorders. Or look at the exploding number of sex scandals related to the church, the workplace, the home. It seems that everywhere we turn, we confront the reality that we cannot stand and do not know how to relate to the temple God created to house our hearts and minds.

But what does any of this have to do with prayer? Remember that prayer is about listening, paying attention, noticing what is really there, being aware of the truth. So what is the truth of our condition in the world, a truth that we must discern through the cloud of negativity described above?

God did not make us disembodied spirits. We do not float around in the ether communing with one another via telepathic thoughts. We are formed and made in material bodies that come from the dust of the earth. This is what God did and does again and again every time a baby is conceived. Furthermore, we are not asexual beings like the amoeba or the mushroom. Rather, we exist in sexual bodies just like the vast majority of creatures on earth. Again, God did this; I am not making it up.

Therefore, just as we are able to reach out to God with our hearts and minds (notice how even this language is physical), we are able to reach out to God with and through our bodies. For it is through our bodies that we see and experience beauty, love, joy, and peace. It is through our bodies that we know the ecstasy of the divine fire burning in our hearts as we enter more deeply into prayer. It is through our bodies that we meet the One who came in a body to dwell among us, heal us, and help us to know God.

SPECIAL TRAVELING COMPANIONS

Finding a historical figure to help us with this part of the journey is not easy because of the problems I have already discussed: The church and the body have not gotten along well. Unfortunately most of the saints of our faith subscribed to the notion that their bodies were somehow bad. Therefore, this chapter requires a slightly different approach.

As our traveling companions I will call upon scripture, specifically the Song of Solomon, and a so-called negative historical example, two of the most famous lovers in Christian history: Abelard and Heloise. This couple's powerful love mirrored the love described in the Song of Solomon; however, because of the unfortunate views of the body pervading their culture, this love was not seen as a reflection of the divine but rather as an evil that brought them to a tragic end. These resources will be of use as we venture into the realm of incarnated prayer.

Our bodies are incredibly powerful. They are able to evoke emotions, thoughts, and feelings that overwhelm us—sweep us off our feet, the old saying goes. This power may explain why so much negativity has been directed at the body. We have a vague sense that we are always on the verge of being mastered by something beyond our control.

The Song of Solomon uses the body's power to illustrate the power of the ultimate love relationship, the relationship between the Creator and the created. The bride seeks "him whom my soul loves" (Song of Sol. 3:1). She rises out of bed and is drawn to search "about in the city" (Song of Sol. 3:3), so great is her yearning. Clearly the desire and love described are set aflame by the beauty of the human body, a beauty that reflects the beauty of all creation: "My beloved is to me a bag of myrrh that lies between my breasts. My beloved is to me a cluster of henna blossoms in the vineyards of En-gedi" (Song of Sol. 1:13-14).

If we can set aside our negative prejudices about the body for a moment, we can see that by expressing the power of bodily experience, the author of this book conveys the power of divine love. Thus, rather than rejecting these powerful feelings, we need to recognize that they are actually opportunities for prayer.

HELOISE AND ABELARD

Heloise and Peter Abelard lived in the twelfth century and met in Paris. He was a rising brilliant theologian, and she was the niece of a wealthy French nobleman. Abelard fell in love with Heloise, and they began a torrid affair after Abelard convinced her uncle to allow him to live in the uncle's house as Heloise's tutor. She eventually became pregnant. Although the couple desired to keep their relationship a secret, Heloise's uncle began talking about their private marriage. At this point, Heloise denounced her family, and Abelard arranged for her to live in a convent. Enraged by this turn of events, the uncle had Abelard castrated. Subsequently Abelard became a monk. Much of what we know of their relationship comes from the letters Heloise and Abelard exchanged after their separation.

In their letters, Heloise and Abelard refer to the Song of Solomon to describe how they feel about each other. However, rather than seeing their feelings as a reflection of divine love, the premise of the Song, they often see those feelings as sinful lust. Heloise writes:

> In my case, the pleasures of lovers which we shared
> . . . can scarcely be banished from my thoughts. . . .
> Even during the celebration of the Mass, when our
> prayers should be purer, lewd visions of those plea-
> sures take such a hold upon my unhappy soul that
> my thoughts are on their wantonness instead of on
> prayers. (*Letters of Abelard and Heloise,* 133)

Yet what if we were to view our bodies as Solomon's song sees them—as vehicles for knowledge of the divine? What if we were to embrace the power of our bodies in prayer? What if we were to bring the attention of contemplation to our physical beings? Much of the sin of the body comes not, I feel, from the inherent power of the body but rather from ignoring or suppressing our feelings and then unconsciously acting out in negative ways.

The tragedy of domestic violence illustrates what I'm describing. Men (in over 90 percent of domestic violence cases) use their bodies to commit horrible crimes against women, in large measure because they are out of touch with their feelings and their bodies. In one effective treatment program for offenders, men learn that the solution to their violence is to pay attention to their bodies, to their feelings, to their reactions in different situations. They learn how to defuse the feelings of rage and replace them with feelings and experiences of self-care and love. In religious language, they are taught how to use their bodies to experience the love of God.

Bodily prayer brings to our bodies the same attitude that we brought to our thoughts in the previous practices. It is about listening, paying attention, quietly watching. In this space of silence, the body becomes like a temple. We begin to pray into our feelings and to see our feelings as prayer. As with our previous practices, it is helpful to have some form for this prayer, and so I now turn to a discussion of specific bodily prayer practices.

BREATHING AS PRAYER

Any bodily prayer practice, including breathing, begins just as our other practices began—with listening. Notice how you feel as you approach the practice: What do you experience as you bring your attention to your body? Furthermore, what is your intention as you begin to pray? As you encountered the full content of your mind when you began silent prayer or the Jesus Prayer, so too you will encounter your attitudes and feelings about your body when you begin bodily prayer. Maybe you are ashamed of your body, or you believe that your bodily feelings are evil. Maybe you will notice all your aches and pains. Or perhaps you will simply become aware of the fact that you ignore your body most of the time. Allowing yourself to notice all these thoughts and feelings is an integral component of the prayer practice.

Just as Abelard and Heloise longed for each other all the more once they were separated, so too our bodies will cry out for our attention the more we ignore them. Illness, fantasies, or unhealthy behavior may all signal the body's need for attention. So begin your prayer by dedicating your feelings about your body to God. Express to God your intention to know God's love through your physical being. In this dedication of intention you connect mind and body; you ask God to awaken your mind through the life-giving energy within the body. The biblical author tells us: "I slept, but my heart was awake. Listen! my beloved is knocking" (Song of Sol. 5:2). With this marking of your intention to awaken to God, you are ready to begin.

Breathing may seem like a ridiculous focus for prayer. Yet most of us do not breathe in a manner conducive to experiencing God. We restrict our breath, often taking shallow, quick gulps of air. Yet scripture presents breath as the fundamental metaphor for the Spirit of God, suggesting the breath's special significance. It is through breath that God gives life (Gen. 2:7), and it is through breath that Jesus bestows the Spirit (John 20:22).

In the Song of Solomon, the wind plays an important role: When the young woman wants to attract her lover, she invokes the winds: "Awake, O north wind, and come, O south wind! Blow upon my garden that its fragrance may be wafted abroad. Let my beloved come to his garden, and eat its choicest fruits" (Song of Sol. 4:16). Breathe, and God will come and enter into you.

Breathing as prayer is similar to silent prayer, and it can be done at any time, for we are always breathing. The practice is simple: Take some time to notice how you breathe. Sit upright in a silent place. Draw your attention to your breath. Most of us breathe with our chest only, yet our deepest breath comes when we breathe from our abdomen, allowing our diaphragm to expand fully. As our stomach muscles expand, we breathe in, and as they contract we breathe out. Watch a baby and you'll see this natural deep breathing in action. Set aside some time to practice breathing like this; you might begin with ten to twenty minutes. Breathe slowly; breathing too quickly can cause you to hyperventilate. Pay attention to the sensation of completely filling your lungs and slowly releasing the air. You may find breathing differently hard at first. Ask God to fill you with the spirit of life.

After a few minutes you may notice that you are more alert and awake. Or you may notice the opposite: You feel exhausted, burned out, in pain, or in need of healing. In either case, these feelings give you information about yourself and your relationship to the divine.

In apophatic prayer (chapter 4), bringing your attention back to a word helps to reveal God's presence in your life. Similarly, in breath prayer, bringing your attention back to your breath allows you, over time, to more fully experience God's presence in your life. For the act of breathing opens that quiet space inside yourself where you can begin to notice the Holy Spirit coursing through your veins.

Breath prayer is a solitary type of body prayer. What about group practices? There are many kinds of body prayer practices that lend themselves to groups; here we will look at one.

BODY SCULPTURE PRAYERS

In body sculpture prayer, you use your body to express a prayerful response to scripture. It is best done in a large room where the group can sit comfortably and still have enough extra space in which to form the body sculptures. If the group desires, set up an altar in the space where sculptures will be created.

The leader of the group chooses a Bible passage and reads it aloud twice while the group listens in silence. Then the leader picks one word from the passage and reads it aloud twice. After the word is read, whoever feels called to create a sculpture goes to the open space and forms a posture in response to the word. The person holds that posture. For example, if the word were *joy*, someone might stand with arms outstretched as a posture expressing the feeling of joy.

Several people from the group may want to form a sculpture, but not everyone needs to go up for each word. Once several people have taken poses, the result is a beautiful living tableau, a prayerful rendition of the word.

When the leader senses that all who want to form a sculpture have done so, he or she reads the word again. This signals everyone to return to their seats. The process is then repeated for several different words. After all the words have been read and formed, the group can reflect silently and then spend a while discussing the experience.

This bodily version of *lectio divina* allows us to pray into the words of the passage using our bodies. As we form the sculptures and watch the shapes arise, we begin to see and hear God speaking to us out of the passage. The multiple layers and levels of meaning in the scripture come to life literally before our eyes.

Forming the sculptures offers the experience of incarnating the Word. How do these words of God feel in our bodies? What are the responses to these words that God is calling out of us? When our prayers take bodily form, we can begin to know God with our entire being.

VESSELS OF THE HOLY

Experiencing our bodies as vessels for the divine transforms our relationship with our bodies, and we become aware of certain questions about our bodies. What if we were to take our bodily relationships seriously as powerful gifts from God? What if we were to take seriously the powerful feelings present in our bodies as positive reflections of the power and presence of God in our lives? Wouldn't we want to treat our bodies and our bodily relationships with reverence and care as vessels of the Holy?

As we begin to answer these questions, our attention is drawn ever more toward God. We see our every feeling as a pulse of the spirit of life within us, and our desire to treat these feelings with the attitude of prayer grows. I think Abelard and Heloise got into so much trouble because Abelard began their affair frivolously but soon discovered that he was caught in the grip of something much more powerful. Like the couple in the Song of Solomon, these lovers became intoxicated with the power of the love of God, and yet they did not see or treat their feelings as a reflection of the sacred.

Understanding that our feelings of love and desire can contain the love of God changes our attitude toward these feelings. We begin to treat them with the respect they deserve without shame or guilt. We realize that we can pray with and through our bodies.

NINE

WALKING TOWARD GOD
The Journey Made Visible

*As our physical bodies move
through space, our minds move too.
And as our minds move,
God can enter into our beings
because movement
creates space and new possibilities.*

$\mathscr{B}$y now our life with God has encompassed all aspects of our being: heart, mind, and body. Yet "who we are" does not remain static. We move and change and grow. Our life is a four-dimensional process—a movement through both time and space.

In the introduction I talked about the life of prayer as a journey, and this is indeed a popular metaphor for the spiritual life, which is often referred to as the spiritual path. Appropriately there are prayer practices that embrace this image of journey and require our bodies to move through space as a means toward encountering God. In this chapter I will introduce two such practices and discuss the concept of spiritual development, an important notion in the life of prayer.

The practices in this chapter are not associated with any specific historical figure because they developed simultaneously in many different communities. Both practices involve walking, being on a journey. The first is the practice of the slow walk, and the second is the labyrinth.

ON A JOURNEY

The man at the prayer retreat was struggling with many difficult issues in his life. He wasn't sure that he was in the right job. He was concerned about his children's health. Nothing felt right, and he wanted answers from God. He wanted all to be better now; he, like most of us when we are in pain, wanted a magic bullet or pill to fix what ailed him.

So he came to pray. However, as he sat in silence the answer didn't come. God didn't fix his problems. And the longer this went on, the more frustrated and upset he

NOTE: The appendix offers step-by-step instructions for practicing walking prayers individually or with a group.

became. This prayer thing wasn't working; he wasn't getting the solutions he needed and expected. Maybe we, the retreat leaders, didn't know what we were doing.

On the last morning of the retreat, feeling frustrated and a bit angry, this man decided to take a walk. Maybe he would feel better after getting out a bit, moving around in the beautiful sunshine of early spring. As he strolled through the quiet neighborhood, no longer expecting much in the way of guidance or answers, suddenly a voice in his head spoke to him, "You are on a journey."

Later when he told the whole group about this experience, he described the emotions that accompanied this realization as joy, relief, and excitement. His life, a claustrophobic hell of problems and discomfort just moments before, was transformed into a vast horizon of limitless possibilities. Yes, his situation as it currently stood was hard and uncomfortable, but now a new dimension had been added—the possibility of change and renewal.

We are on a journey.

Why is the metaphor of journey so common in describing the spiritual life? What is compelling about this image? In part I think it arises because we are creatures who grow and develop and move about in the world. We do not live lives rooted in one spot like trees; nor do we stay the same size and shape all our lives like single-celled creatures. Our life is a movement through time and space, and in fact many people have asserted that without this movement, we would not be able to form personalities and identities.

This motion provides for us new view and vision. We perceive that there is something else just over the horizon; life looks different at age ten and age twenty and age eighty; change and new possibilities exist. Furthermore, we know that our relationships, whether with people, fields of knowledge, jobs, or hobbies, can deepen and develop over time, becoming richer and more complex (this can happen in both "good" and "bad" relationships!).

We are on a journey.

The promise of deepening and enrichment is no less true of our relationship with God. If God is indeed a living being, then our relationship with that being is subject to change, growth, and development. Now this notion, although in some ways obvious, is actually quite tricky and, within the church, can be a subject of divisive debate. Deep down, many people have developed the image of a static, unchanging relationship with God. Consciously or unconsciously, they believe that once they "believe in Jesus," there is nothing more to do or develop or understand. Like my friend on the retreat who felt he deserved answers from God because he was a good Christian, we shape our relationship with God into a fixed entity that should provide certain results, including a one-way trip to heaven at the end of our lives.

If you don't believe me, just try talking about your developing prayer life in a church community. You may soon find, especially in mainline church communities, that some people accuse you of being a spiritual snob. They think you are acting "more holy" than they or implying you are "more spiritual" than they are. Such comments point to a lack of realization that development is part of the spiritual life, just as it is part of any activity. Now "development" does not mean that we have to achieve certain things in our prayer life in order to get into heaven. Developing our spiritual life does mean our relationship with God can become richer and fuller, and as we grow in that relationship, we can begin to experience heaven before we get there!

Understanding that development is part of the spiritual life opens up a whole realm of possibility: God is not finished with us yet! We can relax into the present, knowing that tomorrow holds the reality that God's graces are new every morning. Whatever our situation may be now, transformation is indeed possible; the world and our place in it are not static; rather they are dynamic, ever-moving, ever-growing, ever-reaching toward the new heaven and the new earth.

JOURNEY IN THE HISTORY OF OUR FAITH

Incorporating the concept of journey and development into the process of prayer has ancient roots. For one reason, the central stories of our faith are stories of movement. In the Exodus, the people of God move from one land to another as a demonstration of the movement from slavery to freedom. Then, as the people of Israel fall away from true worship of God, this movement reverses when they are taken into exile and return to a state of subjugation.

Jesus was always on the move. As he taught and healed, he moved back and forth across the Sea of Galilee or from one district to another. Then Jesus "set his face to go to Jerusalem" (Luke 9:51), as he prepared to move toward events we now observe during Holy Week. Even after his death, Jesus taught while traveling. The "walk to Emmaus" (Luke 24:13-35) has become a key parable to describe the process of recognizing the risen Christ in our lives.

These stories, along with the recognition of development as part of the spiritual life, led to the creation of prayer practices involving movement. Early in the life of the church, one of the most common of these practices was the pilgrimage. Christians were encouraged to make a sacred journey to Jerusalem at some point in their lives. This trip symbolized the baptismal transformation of dying and rising to new life. As the pilgrim made the trip to the city where Jesus died and was resurrected, he or she would spiritually shed old identities and take on the new identity of a believer. Then, upon the return home, that individual symbolically brought back this new identity to the world. As time went on, extreme forms of this practice developed, including the idea that one should make the entire trip crawling on one's knees.

Once monastic communities began to develop, the architecture of a monastery often allowed the monks to spend time in walking prayer. The cloister, or walkway around a central courtyard, was a place where monks or nuns could walk endlessly in circles, meditating on their relationship with God.

What is happening in these practices? As our physical bodies move through space, our minds move too. And as our minds move, God can enter into our beings because movement creates space and new possibilities. The movement of our bodies both mimics and allows for the movement of our relationship with Jesus. This is the story of the road to Emmaus. As the disciples walked and listened, their hearts burned within them (Luke 24:32), and they were opened to the recognition of the risen Christ.

WALKING PRAYER

A simple practice for individuals or groups is slow walking. This prayer practice can slow the commotion in our mind, thus opening our self to God. To try this practice, decide on an amount of time to spend in prayer. Since this practice involves walking, you will need to select a route. If you are inside, you could walk in a circle—preferably clockwise—around a room, an easy configuration, especially in the group setting. If you are outside, then perhaps picking a route in advance is not as essential.

As with all our practices, start by addressing God and stating your intention to know God's presence through the practice. Then begin to walk very slowly and continue for your set time. That is all. At first, what may seem slow to you will still be quite fast. Every few steps, slow your pace even more. Try to reach a point where you are taking at least fifteen to thirty seconds for every step (this will seem like an incredibly long time). As you walk, pay attention to the movement of your feet. Feel them on the ground. Feel as one leaves the ground, moves through space, and then touches the earth again. Allow your mind to begin to move as slowly as your body.

At first the exact opposite will happen. Your mind will begin to race. You will notice how full it is, how it runs like one of those bird-shaped lawn ornaments whose wings spin in the breeze as the bird goes nowhere. No wonder we rarely notice God; there is no space for the Spirit to speak to us!

You may notice your desires. You feel the need to move more quickly, or you have an itch, or there is something you just have to talk about. Perhaps you become aware of how anxious you are. Allow these desires and feelings to wash over you and notice how they eventually subside.

Someone once told me about developing an itch on his nose as he walked. He decided he would scratch the itch, but he would move his hand as slowly as he was walking. By the time his hand reached his nose, the itch was gone.

As our bodies move slowly through physical space, our hearts and minds open to the vastness of spiritual space. The kingdom of God draws near. Usually we are moving too quickly to see and feel that presence. However, as we pray, with each incredibly slow step we move into that space of the eternal present, just as the children in C. S. Lewis's *Chronicles of Narnia* stepped into a new world as they ventured into the mysterious wardrobe.

Slow walking increases our awareness, which in turn heightens our ability to notice God. As we become familiar with this prayer practice, we perceive our surroundings more fully. We become aware of how quickly we are moving, and the desire to slow down and watch for God grows in our hearts. God begins to speak to us out of the content of our lives, and the knowledge that we are indeed on a journey into the Holy grows.

In a group setting, after the actual practice of slow walking, spend some time debriefing the experience. The group can support and encourage any who find the practice difficult or frustrating, and people can share what they are noticing as they do the practice. Try the prayer regularly over a span of several months, and see what changes people report in their lives and their relationship with God. Group members may begin to understand and recognize that they are on a journey.

THE LABYRINTH

Earlier I talked about the pilgrimage to Jerusalem and how this became one type of movement prayer in the early church. In 638 C.E. Jerusalem was conquered by the Muslim armies, and from this point on, such a pilgrimage became increasingly difficult. By the time of the Crusades in the Middle Ages, it was all but impossible. This historical change prompted development of the Christian practice of the labyrinth.

Labyrinths have been used as a tool for prayer in many traditions; some are more than four thousand years old. A labyrinth is not a maze. Rather it is a single path that has been wrapped around itself in a symmetrical formation. Labyrinths may be round, square, or triangular. A labyrinth has a single entrance. After entering, a walker follows the winding path to the center and then exits by following the same path in reverse. Once traveling to Jerusalem was no longer practical, Christian communities began to build labyrinths as substitutes for the actual pilgrimage. The path of the labyrinth traditionally was carved in the stone floor of a church or monastery.

In the practice of the labyrinth, you walk the path to the center of the figure and then return to the exit at your own pace. The journey can take a few minutes or an hour. You can think of the prayer as divided into three phases. In the first phase, you are walking toward God—the center of the labyrinth. In this phase you shed all that is keeping you from union with the Creator. The second phase symbolizes union with God as you arrive at the center of the labyrinth. Finally in the third phase, as you exit from the center, you are going with God back out into the world. As with the actual journey to Jerusalem, this process imitates the dying and rising to new life in Christ, the story at the heart of our faith.

The biggest challenge for doing the prayer of the labyrinth is finding a labyrinth! Although this prayer is gaining in popularity, finding one is still rather difficult. Few churches in the country have one permanently installed; however, more churches do have access to a portable labyrinth, one or several pieces of canvas with a painted path. Kits for creating a labyrinth are also available.

If you can locate a portable labyrinth, you need a big room in which to spread it out or a suitable outdoor space (be sure outdoor use is permissible; I got in trouble once for returning one with grass on it!). If you are able to find a permanently installed labyrinth, plan and schedule when you can use it. Although you can walk the labyrinth alone, gathering a group to walk together adds a wonderful dimension to the practice.

Begin with a short time of silence. Then begin walking, leaving some space between each person as individuals enter the labyrinth. Everyone should proceed at his or her own pace. If one person needs to pass another, the first does so gently and in silence. Upon reaching the center, each person may spend as much time there as desired and then begin the journey outward.

As you walk the labyrinth, draw your attention to God. Watch your thoughts. You might wish to let your mind wander, or you may want to actively pray. You could recite scripture silently, or you could fashion some questions for the journey. For example, for the journey toward the center, ask yourself what you need to let go of or what obstacles prevent a closer relationship with God. Once in the middle, you might ask God to enter your life more fully. Then on the way out of the labyrinth, you might ask what areas of your life could become more filled with God's presence.

During the entire journey, pay attention to your body as it moves through space. Look at the others as they walk.

·

Notice how it feels to be on the spiritual path with yourself and others. How is God speaking to you through your body? When all group members have finished walking, take time to share observations and experiences with one another.

Each time we walk the labyrinth, our experience is different. This variation reflects the truth of spiritual development and journey. We are always walking toward God, and at each point along the road we notice new and different things. The prayer of the labyrinth helps us to realize that truth. It also allows us to fully enter into the process of coming to God and then going out into our lives in the company of our Creator.

In our life with God, we are indeed on a journey.

TEN

PRAYING IN NATURE
Contemplation and Creation

TRAVELING COMPANION
Saint Francis of Assisi

*Saint Francis realized that the love and
glory of God are in everything and for everything.
If we realized the same,
we would never disrespect, degrade,
or destroy one another and
the world as we have in
the past and continue to do today.*

The previous chapter took up the topic of journey. Just as our spiritual lives are a journey, so too in this book we are on a journey, a journey of exploration into the nature of a life with God. Our travels began with our hearts and minds reaching into the unknown, seeking union with the One Who Is. We then moved to an examination of our bodies, for we are created beings who experience God through our senses. This led to a discussion of how we can pray as our bodies move through space and time.

In these last chapters, I come to the recognition that we do not exist in isolation like one marooned on a desert island or floating through the vast emptiness of space. We are creatures—part of a created world—and we share this world with other creatures, both human and nonhuman. Thus any discussion of life with God would be incomplete without reflecting upon how we pray as we relate to these others. In this chapter I will discuss praying with nature, and the next chapters offer an examination of prayer via our way of life, and finally, the practice of community.

EXPERIENCING GOD IN CREATION

When I ask people where and how they experience God, most of them will tell me a story about being in a natural environment. Whether a sunset, the view from a mountain, the silence of the wilderness, the song of a bird, or the power of a storm, people see, hear, and feel God through God's creation. This is no more true now than when the Bible was being written. As I mentioned in the chapter on creativity, creation is a cornerstone of the biblical witness.

NOTE: The appendix offers step-by-step instructions for practicing prayers in nature individually or with a group.

In this chapter, we'll focus not so much on the act of creation but on the reality of the created world and how God is seen through and reflected in that world.

The psalmist tells again and again how the deeds of God are seen in creation (for example, Ps. 104:24), how the earth moves and melts and is transformed when God appears and acts (Ps. 97:5). We saw in the Song of Solomon how the beauty of God's creation reflected God's love. Jesus used the rhythms of creation—blooming fields (Matt. 6:30), harvesting vineyards (Matt. 20:1), bubbling yeast (Matt. 13:33), or sprouting mustard plants (Matt. 13:31)—as material for his parables.

We know God's wisdom, power, and love through God's works. Just like Job, when we gaze into the sky, we are asked: "Do you know the balancings of the clouds, the wondrous works of the one whose knowledge is perfect?" (Job 37:16). People commonly refer to areas of unspoiled wilderness as "God's country," reflecting the prevalence of this vision of God in nature. However, recognizing God's presence in nature does not mean that the things of creation *are* God (some theologians and church folks get worried about such confusion occasionally). Obviously a tree is not God: first of all, a tree doesn't do much other than be a tree; and second, when the tree dies, we do not say that God is dead. God speaks *through* God's creation, and we who seek God are able to experience, through nature, the saving love of Jesus "through whom are all things" (1 Cor. 8:6).

SAINT FRANCIS OF ASSISI

The person who, perhaps more than anyone, can help us with our vision of God in nature is Francis Bernardone, the man who became Saint Francis of Assisi. Born some time around 1182, Francis's story is similar to that of many great mystics. His early life was one of comfort and wealth; however, he eventually had a conversion experience in which he felt called by God to leave his former existence and devote his life to Jesus.

For Francis, the guiding principles of his new reality were simplicity, poverty, caring for the sick and poor, and a vision of God's love that allowed him to see the divine in all creation. Francis has been called a "nature mystic" because of this ability to see the unifying power of God in every creature (*Saint Francis: Nature Mystic,* 9).

Imagining what it is like to spend time with any spiritual master, including Saint Francis, is difficult. We learn something of Francis as we meet him in the stories of *The Little Flowers of St. Francis of Assisi,* a book written at least fifty years after he died. In this book we find the famous tales of Francis preaching to birds, negotiating with a wolf, and multiplying vineyards. As modern people, we tend to dismiss these tales as fabricated legends. However, if we do this, I think we miss the point of the stories, which originated with people who lived with and knew Francis. As with all historical figures, we must ask: What spiritual experience lies behind the tales? What did people see and feel when they were with the poor little saint?

"We are one in Christ." How many times have you heard this in church? It is a statement repeated so often that most people don't give it any thought. If we do consider these words and then look around our communities, our families, our world, we must come to the conclusion that this declaration perhaps represents nothing more than an abstract concept. Every day we confront the reality of division in almost every conceivable manner—we are divided by class, race, opinion, gender, generation, and culture—and this is just people. The best way to become labeled a radical environmentalist is to start talking about our unity with the plants and animals. Yet Saint Francis,

> as he passed along [the road], full of fervor, . . . lifted up his eyes and saw certain trees hard by the road and upon them an almost infinite number of birds. St. Francis marveled at this sight and said to his companions, "You shall await me here on the road, and I will go and preach to the birds, my sisters." (*Little Flowers*, 36)

The story continues with Francis preaching to the birds about the glory and love of God, and when he finishes, the birds fly off in the four directions of the compass, signifying the spread of the gospel to the whole world by Saint Francis and his friars.

When people encountered Saint Francis, "full of fervor," they saw someone in whom the unity of all in Christ was not an abstract concept but a living reality. Francis saw and experienced God in everything around him. The birds were his sisters, the sun his brother, the earth his mother. When he meditated upon the natural world, he saw the glory of God all around him; he could preach to the birds because he "devoutly praised the Creator in them" (*Little Flowers*, 36, 117–18, 37). This is the practice of praying in nature.

As we contemplate the glory of creation, the realization that we are all connected in God starts to take hold in our hearts and minds. On some level we interact with every creature on this planet. We breathe the air that has been in the lungs of others around the globe; we take in the oxygen from the leaves of plants and the water in the sea. Saint Francis realized that the love and glory of God are in everything and for everything. If we realized the same, we would never disrespect, degrade, or destroy one another and the world as we have in the past and do today.

So profound was his understanding of peace and love in a unified world that Francis went into the woods to make peace with a wolf who was killing both animals and people in a town called Gubbio. Whereas we might head into the forest with guns to kill the wolf, Francis approached the wolf unarmed and addressed him as "friar," the same term used to address a brother monk.

> "Friar wolf," [says Francis], "you do much damage in these parts . . . for which cause you merit the gallows as a thief and most iniquitous murderer. . . . But I desire, friar wolf, to make peace between you and them [the townspeople] so that you may no more offend them and that they may forgive you."(*Little Flowers*, 48)

Francis promised the wolf that he would be fed by the people of the town so that he would no longer have to kill anything, and following their discussion, the wolf went into town with Francis to seal the bargain. It was then through the "strangeness of the miracle" that the towns-people came to know the blessing and the glory of God (*Little Flowers*, 49).

OPPORTUNITIES FOR PRAYER IN NATURE

Those of us who have regular access to the beauty of the natural world may easily forget, or at least find hard to appreciate, the power of praying in nature. If I ever had any doubt about the ability of the natural world to help create a spiritual experience, this doubt was dispelled after my wife and I invited a group of inner-city youth from New York to come to our farm in Vermont for a retreat.

These young people had never seen a lawn. They had never seen the stars because they had never been anywhere that got dark at night. When I told them to stay on the grass around our house and not go into the vegetable gardens, they looked at me and said, "What vegetables?"

On the second day of our retreat, we decided to take the youth for a hike, something else they had never done. We selected a hike near our farm where a short but strenuous walk up a hill culminated at the top in a 360-degree view of the Green Mountains. One of the girls was obviously in poor physical condition and had asthma. To make matters worse, she had forgotten her inhaler; it was a real challenge to get her up that hill.

She and I reached the top long after the others had left. She was exhausted and out of breath. We simply sat silently on the rocks of the summit, gazing out at the valleys spread below us. Later that night the group shared experiences of the day, and the young woman said, with great enthusiasm, feeling, and a huge smile on her face, "That hike today, now *that* was a spiritual experience."

When the youth left the following afternoon, I could see how touched they had been by spending time in contact with the natural world. When they had first arrived, they had difficulty talking about God or their spiritual lives; now, just a few short days later, it seemed that the notion of the divine made more sense to them. They had been touched by the presence of God in nature.

There are multitudes of ways to pray with the natural world. My hope here is not to describe all of them but rather to point in a few directions from which you may proceed on your own. Much like the prayer practice of creativity, the possibilities are endless once you begin to explore them.

The natural world surrounds you, and you can begin this prayer by noticing this world anew. The part of the country where I now live offers up some of the most beautiful sunsets and sunrises I have ever seen. Yet when I talk to people here about these beautiful celestial displays, what I sometimes hear is that they have stopped looking at them. So you can start by looking around. Perhaps you already take walks in a park or around your neighborhood. The next time you do this, look up; see the sky. Look at the trees or the flowers or even the weeds that struggle to grow through cracks in the sidewalk. Listen for the birds. Then draw your attention to the One who created all this. Ask God to make you aware of the presence of the Holy in all things. Realize that God is all around you. Ask yourself, *Do I see Christ in the birds and hear the Spirit in the wind?* As you ask the question, allow yourself to be drawn into the silence of prayer. Listen for the voice of Jesus.

Your relationship with food holds another opportunity for prayer with nature. Unfortunately more and more people relate to food the way a car relates to gas: They zoom into the service station, fill up, and zoom off. But your eating and meal preparation present rich avenues for prayer. As you prepare and eat a meal, take the time to think about your food. Everything you are eating came from the earth. Everything was nourished by the sun and the rain and the care of a person who spent many hours growing the food so that you might be sustained. Pray into these realities. Feel the love and the care that live in each bite you take. Allow gratitude to arise in you. This is what Francis felt as he wrote:

Praised be my Lord for brother wind,
And for the air and clouds and fair and every kind
of weather,
By the which Thou givest to Thy creatures
nourishment. (*Little Flowers*, 117)

Maybe this attention will prompt you to notice and change unhealthy eating habits. Perhaps you will realize that you desire to eat more slowly, or you may want to take the time to eat and prepare fresher and more nourishing food. These desires reflect the presence of a loving God, of One who formed you from the earth and nourishes you with the earth.

A third way to pray with nature is to practice another type of prayer in a natural setting. You will likely find the presence of the natural world enhances and deepens your other prayer techniques. For example, while on a solitary hike, I often stop and spend time in silent prayer. I also use bike rides as a time to practice the examen after a Sunday service or a planning meeting. During these times of prayer, the presence of God in nature supports and a reinforces my other prayer practices.

As you practice a variety of prayers in nature, you will find yourself more drawn to prayer whenever you are outside, when you are cooking, or any time you encounter the natural world. This tendency often develops when people are on retreat in a beautiful natural setting. As the retreat progresses, people spend more time outside walking in nature, sitting on the grass, or drawing a tree. The more the retreatants pray, the more they are drawn into the created world where they can hear God speaking to them.

Praying with Nature— Individual or Group Practice

We've looked at general ways of praying with nature, but what about specific practices, especially ones that can be taught in group settings? Again, there are many possibilities, so here I will describe just one that is simple and can be adapted to any setting. The following would be the instructions given to the participants.

The practice involves a deep examination of a natural object—a leaf, a flower, a tree, the grass, the sky, anything. In this prayer a certain amount of time is set aside during which you will examine your item in silence, after you have begun by noting your intention and desire to see God in all.

We rarely take the time to really look at things. So in this practice, you have the opportunity to look deeply. Examine the veins on a leaf. Appreciate the shape, the texture, the color of a tree branch. Allow your mind to imagine how this object came into being, its various stages of growth. What other creatures have benefited from the shade of the tree? Realize that you are breathing the oxygen produced by the grass beneath your feet.

When Saint Francis looked at the turtledoves, he saw the glory of God. The miracle and beauty of that vision are the direction in which this practice points. As you begin to examine a flower intently, you may find your mind transported to other thoughts and ideas. You may realize how much you appreciate the world, your life, other people. You may find that God is speaking to you about something that has nothing to do with the flower. During the silence be aware of these thoughts and feelings, but also continue to examine your piece of the natural world. When the time of reflection comes to an end, express your gratitude to God.

If you are practicing this prayer on your own, you may want to journal about your experience. If you are in a group, you'll find that setting provides an excellent place to share your observations and experiences. A group leader can also link this practice to the practice of creativity by giving group members time to draw in response to their examination.

Whether or not we believe the literal content of the stories about Saint Francis is not really the point of reading them. Rather these stories reveal a humble man in whom people saw someone who inhabited the world of the psalms in which the mountains skip, the hills sing, and all creation praises God. As we practice praying to God in nature, we too begin to inhabit this reality, and we realize that we live our life in a realm where everything whispers to us of the divine.

ELEVEN

PRAYER AND LIFE IN THE WORLD
The Rubber Meets the Road

TRAVELING COMPANIONS
The Beguines

*Our whole existence is transformed
as we begin to seek God in all that
we do and in all that we are.
Our lives are no longer
compartmentalized into times
for prayer and times for other things.*

*B*eing in nature is only one small component of living in the material world. We spend the majority of our time taking care of ourselves and our families, working, buying things, watching TV, and occasionally participating in recreational activities. In this chapter I examine the questions: How do we pray with our lives? What happens when we use our whole existence as a vehicle for prayer? Does the way we live change if we pray into all that we do?

It seems that in developed nations, the practice of prayer has become somewhat disconnected from issues and questions related to our material existence. In this chapter I will attempt to bridge this divide, using several historical figures as reference points. We will revisit briefly all the people with whom we have journeyed so far and then meet a new group, the Beguines.

LESS STUFF

All the traveling companions in this book hold one characteristic in common: The more they prayed, the less stuff they had or needed. Contrary to the contemporary slogan proclaiming the one with the most stuff wins, it seems that the closer to God one becomes, the less one needs, or even desires, material goods. This sense of needing less is closely connected with one particular attribute: trust in God.

Whether it was Saint Francis or the desert mothers and fathers or the pilgrim or Julian of Norwich, the closer each came in relationship to God, the more he or she trusted in God for everything. So as we pray with and into our material situation in the world, we confront the question: Do

NOTE: The appendix offers step-by-step instructions for practicing tithing and The Impossible Project.

we really trust God with our lives—our literal, physical lives? This is a very challenging question. Maybe we trust God with our thoughts and feelings, but what about the material stuff that keeps us fed and housed? And what about our attention and our priorities? As we pray into our lifestyle, we encounter the issue of materialism. What is it that holds our attention—God or stuff?

In late twelfth-century Europe, a religious movement addressing these issues and questions began. Lasting well into the fourteenth century, it consisted of lay communities of women who came to be called the Beguines. They are our companions for this part of our journey.

The women who formed this movement desired to live a life that would "imitate as closely as possible the human life of Christ and his sufferings." They desired to live a life of prayer and simplicity, which they saw as closely connected. Their "emphasis was not on spiritual poverty alone but on a materially simple life-style linked to self-support by the work of their hands" (*Spirituality and History*, 153, 162).

The reason for this choice of lifestyle was not only the desire to imitate Christ but also the desire to trust God and achieve prayerful union with God. The Beguines acted on these desires by establishing communal living situations where they could do simple work, pray, and be of service. As they prayed into their lives, they created an "alternative life-style"; alternative to "the natural order of society" because it "involved a deliberate denial of their [social] background and an acceptance of a way of life that was socially distasteful" (*Spirituality and History*, 163, 150).

In these women, many of whom came from comfortable families in Europe, we witness the basic reality of which Jesus speaks: The more we pray, the more we feel concern for others and the less we worry about our own accumulating. Most of us who have read the Bible at all know this truth in our hearts. Yet for those of us who live in the midst of a powerful materialistic machine, global capitalism, it is a truth easy to forget and hard to live out.

A friend recently tried to do a secret prayer practice during Lent and found out what a strong grip this materialism has on her life. She intended to give away some of her possessions throughout the Lenten season, slowly relieving herself of some of their weight. What she found surprised her. This practice proved to be so challenging that by the time Holy Week rolled around, she felt she had failed in her task. She told me she had learned what a powerful force materialism was in her life and in the life of her family. It became especially clear to her how materialism affected her children, and we talked about how our kids already were captive to the lure of "needing" and getting things.

It was this bondage to the material from which the Beguines were seeking liberation. Because our material desires can be so strong and can invade even our religious institutions, their "emphasis on poverty was often threatening because it . . . tended, implicitly at least, to criticise the wealth of the Church" (*Spirituality and History*, 153). Like our other forms of prayer, praying with our material lives can and will cause upheaval. Just as our minds can revolt against us in silent prayer, so too will our social circles rebel when we begin to question how we are living or what are our material priorities.

But what does reflecting upon our possessions have to do with prayer? What are the practices, and how do these relate to the fundamentals of prayer: bringing ourselves before God, listening to God, noticing God? The most basic individual practice is material giving, which I will address first, followed by giving in the group setting, and one of my favorite practices, The Impossible Project.

TITHING AS A PRAYER PRACTICE

Currently in the United States, the average level of material giving in mainline churches is from 1 to 3 percent of a person's gross income. Obviously these percentages are far below the biblical standard of the tithe—10 percent of gross income. Perhaps some people do not feel their church is worthy to receive their money, but I do not think that this is the main issue. Let us say that you could find a church you would want to support. How is giving 10 percent of your income to the church a prayer practice?

Tithing is a spiritual practice because it requires a level of giving that is hard, and thus it forces us to relate to God as we participate in the practice. Giving away 10 percent hurts; you notice that level of loss. If I make $100 and give away $1, I might not think twice. People let go of $1 all the time, whenever they buy a soda or a cigarette or a lottery ticket. The dollar disappears without a second thought.

However, if I give away $10 per $100, I notice that. Like a phone bill, a car payment, or a substantial purchase, this expenditure is not made lightly. Therefore, when we go to give away money "to God," we run smack up against the question I raised at the beginning of the chapter: Do we trust that God will provide?

When we begin to turn over large amounts of our resources to someone else, we encounter our fears about existence. Will we starve? Will our children go without? Will we become homeless? These are real fears because we see people who live with these outcomes all the time.

When we give away our precious money, we encounter our true feelings about those biblical passages that tell us God will provide and that sound so nice as long as we have money in the bank. The Beguines had to face this fear and this doubt. If they gave away their right to their estate (or their right to marry into someone's estate), would they survive? Or would they simply end up dead in a gutter somewhere in the city, like so many peasants?

Tithing is a prayer practice because it forces us into relationship with God. We must ask God for what we need. Unfortunately most of us don't believe that if we fully commit our lives to God, we will be sustained. Communicating with God about our survival requires trust, which I've already touched on, and an examination of our values and priorities. We begin to examine our fears, ask God for reassurance, and then listen for God's response. What the Beguines found was that they did not starve. In fact, the movement grew and flourished. These women were provided for. What do you notice as your giving increases? Are your basic needs in danger of not being met, or do you find that you are actually just fine?

Another important aspect of the communication process, the prayer process, is an examination of values and priorities. As we begin to give more, we are forced to come face-to-face with the reality of how we use your resources. I know many people who say their financial situation is difficult, yet they spend thousands of dollars a year on cigarettes or alcohol or gambling or new cars or any number of things they do not need. Their lifestyle is far from the one advocated by Jesus, who told Satan that we should "live . . . by every word that comes from the mouth of God" (Matt. 4:4).

This prayer practice challenges us to look at what we regard as important. How do we spend our time and our money? Many of the Beguines traded time at court parties for time in prayer and service. One reason they did not starve was that their change in lifestyle cost less, so scarce resources went farther.

Communicating with God about these concerns leads to the result of all prayer practices—deeper intimacy with Jesus. Much of our material striving is not only about meeting our basic creaturely needs but also about filling the void in our soul that is our separation from God. Advertisers know about this sense of emptiness, and they seek to fill it with their products. Even my ten-year-old son was able to say to me once, "This commercial is stupid, Dad. They say that if you buy this car, your life will be perfect." As we turn our time, resources, and concerns over to God, we find that God begins to fill this void. We slowly come to know that the Holy One is with us in all that we do, all the time. The more we pray with our material lives, the more our thirst for living water is quenched, and we find that we no longer need or want so many material things.

Along with these personal changes, another result of the practice of giving is a change in our relationship with others. The more we pray in this manner, the more we desire to serve others, which leads me to a discussion of how to implement this prayer practice in groups.

COUNTERCULTURAL LIVING AND PRAYING

The Beguines got people's attention because they were living their lives in a manner counter to what society dictated. They were countercultural. Christians in developed countries today typically don't realize that countercultural living always has been the hallmark of Christian communities that have had an enduring impact upon the faith. Unfortunately many contemporary Christians seem to equate being countercultural with listening to Christian radio or not watching certain Hollywood movies. While these behaviors may have some value, they do not get at the heart of how we live our lives in the world.

As we begin to pray with the stuff of our lives, we find, like the Beguines, that we are called to transform our lives based upon God's vision for us and our community. Traditionally, giving as a group practice falls under the category of mission and service; and usually these activities consist of "giving to the poor." Again this is often wonderful work; however, it is not necessarily done from the perspective of a prayer practice. What do I mean?

THE IMPOSSIBLE PROJECT

The hallmark of all our prayer practices is that in some manner they put us at God's disposal. God is in charge, not us. We are there to listen and to notice God's presence; we are not there to have God do our bidding. Usually when a group or church undertakes a service project, the group or church is clearly in charge; the projects are manageable and do not exact too great a toll on those participating. We, not God, are in charge. Like the tithe, a group service project that is a prayer practice demands that the group rely on God for help and guidance. The term I use for this practice is "The Impossible Project."

The Impossible Project cannot be accomplished at a retreat for people coming from different communities or in any other short-term setting; it is a practice for a community of people who are trying to live out their faith in the world. Thus it would be appropriate in any setting within a community built on fairly long-term relationships, such as a church or other Christian organization.

The practice is a prayer, and it requires prayer at every step. Prayer needs to be at the heart of any group that takes it on. So this is a group that sits in silence together; it is a group that does *lectio,* the examen, or the Jesus Prayer together. In short, it is a group seeking a life with God, one that begins to ask how God is calling them to be of service in the world. How is God calling the group to minister to the "least of these" (Matt. 25:40)?

As the group prays together, eventually ideas for service opportunities will begin to emerge in conversation. Some of these ideas will be obvious and fairly straightforward—serving a meal at a soup kitchen or helping with a building project. Some will be more fantastic and improbable—starting a new church, building a youth center. At least a few members of the group will identify these tasks as impossible. The group should pray about all the ideas, perhaps using the examen as a vehicle for this prayer.

Eventually one of the impossible ideas will start to take hold of the group's imagination; members will feel like it is "of God." The prayer practice of the impossible task is to undertake this work—a work that seems ridiculous and impossible. Like tithing, this practice requires that we not only turn to God for help but also examine our understanding of who God is and how God works in the world. It requires us to truly trust God with our lives. For if we really know God as the Creator of the universe, then, in fact, no task is impossible.

It is quite miraculous to be part of the practice of an impossible task. You watch as people begin to know God in a new, vibrant manner. They get funny looks on their faces; they shake their heads. They fall silent more often. As money appears out of nowhere, as resources they never thought they had are put at their disposal, as people with the right skills show up on their doorstep, slowly people realize they are living in God's realm. The reality of the risen Christ among the group becomes too obvious to be ignored.

This is what the Beguines found. It is what the many people who, over the centuries, have turned their whole lives over to God have found. As you pray into the lived reality of the kingdom, your life takes on a new feel, a new taste, and you begin to see miracles everywhere. For as Jesus told his friends many years ago, "The kingdom of God is among you" (Luke 17:21); all we need to do is to pray so that we might see it and live it.

As we conclude this chapter, I hope it is clear how radical life with God truly is. We have moved from mental practices to body prayers to prayer with our lives, discovering the spiritual path is not just about repeating a phrase in our minds. Our lives are no longer compart-mentalized into times of prayer and times for other things. Instead, all that we are and all that we have provide fertile ground for the growth of shalom, the peace of God that passes all understanding.

TWELVE

A PRAYING COMMUNITY
Bringing It All Together

TRAVELING COMPANION
Saint Benedict

A life with God is a life in which
the rhythms of silence and listening
alternate with the rhythms of sharing
and service. By praying with every part
of who we are, we allow the grace that
pours from the well of living water
to trickle through all the aspects
of our being, nourishing and hydrating
that which was parched and dis-eased.

hroughout this book, I have presented most of the prayer practices as if they are tools for "individual spiritual development" (even though these practices can be done in groups). This is a distinctly modern, mostly Western European and American approach. For most of Christian history, prayer practices were tools to be used within a community of prayer. The prayer practice at the heart of all prayer practices was the church, and community was at the core of spiritual experience.

Even when the spiritual life began with a single individual who had a profound realization of God, that person almost immediately formed a community around himself or herself through which that realization could come to fruition in the world. This is true of the people whom we have met in this book, and it makes sense theologically because God desires to work for good in all creation. Salvation is ultimately for God's people, not for just one or two lucky folks. Therefore, this final chapter explores prayer and community or rather, community as prayer. Unlike the other chapters of the book, this one is largely speculative and looks forward to something that just barely exists. What do I mean?

I know many individuals who practice all the prayer techniques discussed so far. They do silent prayer, the Jesus Prayer, prayer in nature, and so forth. Because they are interested in their individual spiritual development, they make prayer practices a regular part of their lives. However, I know of very few churches or communities that are committed, as a group—as an institution—to

NOTE: The appendix offers step-by-step instructions for practicing community prayer.

being a spiritual community. Currently most churches are in flux and struggling in their attempt to define themselves in our so-called postmodern age.

The days of church as a center of social and community life are gone, and so congregations are groping about in the dark trying to decide if they are community centers, old-age homes, spiritual Wal-Marts, or filling stations for the soul. This searching is made all the more difficult by the individualism permeating every aspect of our lives. For people to commit to a life of prayer with a particular community is a huge challenge, maybe impossible.

At the same time, just as there is a tremendous hunger in the world for relationship with God, there is also a tremendous hunger for community. People long to gather with others to share and feel connected and relieve the sense of alienation that permeates their lives. Thus we are at a point in history where we are flirting with new forms of church community. Eventually some of these may lead to the creation of a new type of institution that re-creates the congregation as a center of prayer, as a prayer practice in and of itself. The purpose of this chapter is to point in this direction, to add one more brick in the path toward prayer—deep contemplative prayer—as a community practice. For it is in such a community that a life with God becomes complete: a 24/7 undertaking.

Our guide on this final phase of our journey is someone we have met—Saint Benedict. Although many others have shaped the notion of Christian community over the centuries, he created a form of prayerful institution that has lasted for fifteen hundred years. Thus his model can serve as a jumping-off point for our discussion.

However, this chapter requires a somewhat different form. I cannot give you a community prayer practice to "do." There isn't one form or one technique that will "work." There isn't one church I can tell you to join or even visit. I cannot give you a step-by-step instruction manual on how to turn your youth group, Sunday school class, or Bible study group into a spiritual community.

It *is* possible to present some general themes culled from the wisdom of Benedict with the hope that these can be applied in a unique manner in your particular situation. My working hypothesis is that if enough of these themes are consistently applied in some fashion, in some place, then a new type of spiritual community will arise.

A School for Spiritual Formation

In the chapter on *lectio,* I noted that the primary image used by Benedict in his *Rule* was the creation of a "school for the service of the Lord" (*Rule,* 5). This notion of creating a container within which prayer can flourish is central to understanding community as prayer practice.

The container of the community offers the safe space within which a group of people can give themselves over to God. It is a structured environment within which everything points toward the mind of Christ. As such, this type of school does not resemble our public schools, whose primary goal is the acquisition of knowledge and facts; rather it is a school whose primary purpose is spiritual formation, the creation of persons whose orientation in life is prayer and a reaching out toward God.

Thus the community is not a sterile place that simply serves as a building in which to do prayer practices; rather the practice of living in the community is itself a prayer practice. As we allow ourselves to relate to the life of a community as we would relate to any other prayer technique, we are formed and transformed by God.

This vision of the community differs from the present-day understanding of church as an organization. In the organizational model, I am a member of the institution, and that membership entitles me to take part in certain activities and have certain privileges. Just as with the other prayer practices, relating to community as a prayer practice entitles us to nothing other than giving ourselves over to our Maker. We are not there to use Jesus; we are there to let Jesus use us. To see how *community as the practice of prayer* might be possible, let's examine some key themes held up by Benedict as essential.

HUMILITY, OBEDIENCE, EMPOWERMENT

Benedict felt that the most important ingredient in this process of prayer in community was humility, for it was by humility that one ascended to heaven, and it was by self-exaltation that one descended into hell (*Rule,* 21–22). Humility, a word related to *humus,* which means "the earth," is the notion of being grounded in the reality of who one is before God; it is God who is in charge of our lives—not the other way around.

Benedict is always reminding his community that God is everywhere and knows everything in the hearts and minds of his monks. Given this, it is important to humble oneself before God, always to be attentive to the task of doing the will of God and not the will of the self. Thus humility helps the monks in their individual lives and in the life of the community. The monks are to be humble before God in prayer and also before their fellow monks.

A spirit of humility is to pervade the community, and this is meant to support the tangible awareness of God's constant presence in the life of the monastery.

Closely linked to humility is the notion of obedience—so closely that Benedict names obedience as the first degree of humility. For Benedict, obedience is important because it links directly to the life of Christ; as Christ did the will of his Father, so too the monks, "forsaking their own will," are to do the will of God. True obedience is not slavish outward adherence to rules but obedience done with a right spirit and heart; there must be no "murmuring" against the abbot or against that which one was obeying (*Rule*, 18, 19). As with humility, obedience has an important social as well as individual aspect; the monks are to be obedient to one another so that the will of God can make itself known and flourish in the community.

In the context of our time, the notion of obedience is quite problematic, since we have recently learned of the many abuses that can arise from a perverted use of the concept. To help us understand the word in our current context, I would like to temper the word *obedience* with the word *empowerment.*

At first glance this may seem paradoxical or even impossible; the words appear to denote opposite concepts. However, the link lies in examining to whom we are to be obedient, and by whom we are empowered. The focus of Benedict's obedience was not human authority but God. The problems with the term have evolved from the tendency to substitute human rule for God's rule and the abuse of power resulting from this switch.

God does not wish God's creatures to be squashed under the weight of authoritarian rule or abuse. Rather our

God is the God of Jesus, who heals and liberates the down-trodden as they approach him in faith. As we earnestly come to God, we are not disempowered but rather empow-ered—not by our own will and effort but through the work of God. The obedience Benedict advocated was a desire to obey the will of God in all areas of our lives. This is the obe-dience that results in freedom in Christ and empowers us to share in the salvation Christ offers us.

The sign of our obedience to God—a way to test whether we are practicing "true" obedience—will be growth in the fruits of the Spirit, especially the increase of love and faith in our community.

LISTENING, PRAYER, AND RELATIONSHIP

If humility and obedience are the essential attitudes with which a monk comes before God, then listening is the key activity for monks to engage in once they have taken their place at the feet of Christ. In his prologue, Benedict urges the reader to "incline the ear of your heart" so that the Word of God may be heard (*Rule*, 1). Once again, listen-ing lies at the heart of prayer.

So what was the humble, obedient, silent monk to do? Without question, Benedict's answer was, "Pray." This answer reveals that specific prayer practices are an essential component of the prayer practice of community. Benedict calls prayer the "Work of God," and he admonishes the community that they should "let nothing, therefore, be put before the Work of God" (*Rule*, 36, 62).

In examining Benedict's central focus on prayer, we can also see how important scripture was to the life of the community. Not only is the *Rule* filled with passages from scripture, but scripture was also the focus of the community's prayer life. The Psalms, the Gospels, the Epistles, as well as other parts of the Bible were read and sung during the daily prayer times, and during *lectio divina* scripture was again read and prayed over. Benedict understands that it is through the Word of God that we come to know the Word of God, Jesus, and it is through the process of praying that we will gain this knowledge and have God guide our lives.

Without prayer, the individual monk and the community had lost its purpose and were moving not toward Christ but rather were drifting on the sea of their own wills and ideas. Once Benedict had created this container, this ship in which the community could travel across the sea of chaos to the new Jerusalem, he took great care to discuss both the issue of leadership and relationship within the community.

In Benedict's image of relationship, the brothers treat one another as they would treat Christ. Thus we find the themes of care, hospitality, service, honesty, and trust throughout the *Rule*. Benedict exhorts the monks, "Let the brethren serve one another," and this service is to be made especially visible by the weekly washing of one another's feet (*Rule*, 52, 53). Imagine what would happen if we did this in our local churches.

In all matters of discipline, the underlying goal is always the care of the brother being corrected, and this care is to extend especially to the sick monks or ones who are particularly weak. Guests too should be received like Christ: Their feet should be washed and generous hospitality should be shown to them (*Rule*, 46, 72–74).

Relationships as envisioned by the *Rule* are endowed with a rigorous honesty. The monks are to confess all evil thoughts and sins to the abbot. Benedict also admonishes against "murmuring," both internal and external, because obedience is only true obedience if performed honestly with the attitude of a "cheerful giver" (*Rule*, 26, 19).

Closely allied to this notion of honesty is Benedict's insistence on consequences for inappropriate actions. The care and love the brothers are called to exhibit for one another are not mushy, superficial, or codependent emotions in which they ignore transgressions.

In his lengthy discussions on excommunication, Benedict devises a system of punishments that are much like the modern-day "time-out." A monk is given a time of silence for "pondering" his actions and how he wishes to change his behavior. So, although care is again emphasized, Benedict realizes that problems and issues must not be ignored; rather the abbot or the community needs to go to the heart of the matter and "cut out those faults by the roots" (*Rule*, 45, 10). Again, contrast this approach with the current situation in many churches where negative and dysfunctional behavior run rampant because it would be "unchristian" to confront people about their actions.

This focus on honesty and consequences in relationships is the external manifestation of the internal process of prayer that I have pointed to before. Prayer is often challenging because it confronts us with the honest truth about ourselves and our relationship with God.

When discussing the leadership of the monastery, Benedict carefully applies these notions of relationship. The first thing Benedict makes clear about leadership and community is that the power dynamics in the monastery are mostly horizontal: The monks are all of fairly equal status. Although the abbot is the head of the community, he should "study rather to be loved than to be feared" (*Rule*, 90), and Benedict repeatedly reminds the abbot that he must live under the *Rule* as much as any monk. In fact, the more authority a person carries in the community, the more Benedict insists that person be humble and walk in fear of God's judgment if he should abuse his power.

Thus leaders of the monastery were to be teachers who would inspire by their being and not just by how much they knew. A key aspect of their office was the ability to discern what monks needed in order to grow in the faith. Benedict says that the abbot must "temper all things that the strong may have something to strive after, and the weak may not fall back in dismay" (*Rule*, 91). This inspiring vision fits in with Benedict's understanding of the monastery as a formational community.

Once Benedict had created the container of the monastery and filled it with people who were to relate to one another as if to Christ, he did not suffer under the illusion that this community would immediately function like the kingdom of God. He was aware that the imperfect beings within the community must practice the spiritual life again and again. So Benedict gave the monks a series of practices, or "tools of the spiritual craft," to be employed "unceasingly day and night" (*Rule*, 17). In his *Rule* these tools include: fasting, poverty, detachment from the world, right faith, humility, discernment, and labor. Benedict understood that the spiritual life requires a commitment of time and energy, which brings us to our next topic—stability.

VOW OF STABILITY

Benedict claims that the life of a monk is not harsh, but neither is it easy. It is a life that requires change and giving up old patterns of self-centered behavior. The monks might desire to run from the monastery whenever they encounter God calling them to relinquish some cherished habit or patterns of behavior. Today we see the same phenomenon frequently as people stop praying or leave a church whenever they aren't "getting what they want." Benedict solves this problem with what has come to be called the monastic vow of stability (*Rule*, 5–6).

This vow both assures that the monk has a lifetime to practice the spiritual disciplines and also serves to create the community container within which these disciplines will be practiced. Stability helps to establish the prayerful environment within which a monk's formation would occur.

In our day and age, which stresses individual accomplishment and "moving up the ladder," Benedict's vow of stability challenges any church community, but it is worth reflecting upon. What sort of commitments can a group's members make to one another? Perhaps periods of short-term stability can promote the development of a praying community when long-term commitments are impossible.

Work and Poverty

The final two themes I wish to address are work and poverty. Both of these play important roles in Benedict's *Rule*, and, as with *lectio* and silence, we can see how individual prayer practices link together to form the more complex practice—community life.

For Benedict, it is important that the monks "live by the labor of their hands, as did our Fathers and the Apostles" (*Rule*, 68). The purpose is not only to prevent idleness, which is to be avoided, but also to be a sign that the monks are humble servants who do not live off the labor of others.

This labor is not supposed to earn them great wealth. On the contrary, the monks are to take a vow of poverty and to own nothing, in recognition that all belongs to God and all is shared by the community. Detachment from material items is another spiritual practice Benedict prescribes for his monks. Thus the Benedictine view of work and its relationship to wealth resembles the view we encountered among the Beguines.

Infused with prayer, the life of the monk is centered upon trust in God. His lifestyle is to reflect this trust and is to become a part of his prayer life. Similarly, then, community life as prayer is to be one of simplicity and service. Benedict holds up these themes as vital for a community that wishes to develop people of God.

These are themes that, like all the other prayer practices, challenge us and help us as we strive to live the spiritual life. A modern practice of community might take each theme and examine how to apply it to the particular context of the group. How would the group manifest humility, obedience, or honest relationship? What are the regular prayer practices of the group? Does the group look at the issue of lifestyle as it seeks to be a community of prayer? Is the group forming pray-ers?

I began this book with a chapter on silence and solitude and have ended with a discussion of community. This movement echoes the scriptural movement from the creation out of nothing in Genesis to the revelation of the heavenly kingdom in Revelation 21. Just as God forms a people and then calls them back from the abyss to form them again, our spiritual journey is a journey of recognizing again and again that at times we are lost and then we are found. This process needs both solitude and community because these two settings complement and reinforce our progress along the Way.

A life with God is a life in which the rhythms of silence and listening alternate with the rhythms of sharing and service. By praying with every part of who we are, we allow the grace that pours from the well of living water to trickle through all the aspects of our being, nourishing and hydrating that which was parched and dis-eased.

So begin the adventure, start the journey, follow Jesus. Allow God to transform your mind such that everything you are and everything you encounter speak with the breath of the Spirit.

Let us pray.

REFERENCES

(Titles as cited in the text appear in bold italics below.)

Abelard, Peter and Heloise. ***The Letters of Abelard and Heloise**.* Trans. Betty Radice. New York: Viking Penguin, 1974.

Armstrong, Edward A. ***Saint Francis: Nature Mystic**.* Berkeley, Calif.: University of California Press, 1973.

Benedict. *St. Benedict's **Rule** for Monasteries.* Trans. Leonard J. Doyle. Collegeville, Minn.: Liturgical Press, 1948.

Craine, Renate. ***Hildegard**: Prophet of the Cosmic Christ.* New York: Crossroad Publishing Co., 1997.

French, R. M., trans. *The **Way of a Pilgrim** and the Pilgrim Continues His Way.* San Francisco: Harper San Francisco, 1991.

Hildegard of Bingen. *Hildegard of Bingen: **Mystical Writings**,* ed. Fiona Bowie and Oliver Davies and trans. Robert Carver. New York: Crossroad Publishing Co., 1990.

Ignatius of Loyola. *The **Spiritual Exercises** of St. Ignatius.* Trans. Louis J. Puhl. New York: Vintage Books, 2000.

John of the Cross. *The Ascent of Mount Carmel* in *The Complete Works of Saint John of the Cross.* Trans. and ed. E. Allison Peers. Wheathampstead, Hertfordshire: Anthony Clarke, 1978.

Johnston, William, ed. *The **Cloud** of Unknowing and the Book of Privy Counseling.* New York: Image Books, 1973.

Julian of Norwich. ***Revelation of Love**.* Ed. and trans. John Skinner. New York: Image Books, 1997.

Merton, Thomas, trans. *The **Wisdom of the Desert**: Sayings from the Desert Fathers of the Fourth Century.* New York: New Directions, 1960.

Sheldrake, Philip. ***Spirituality and History**: Questions of Interpretation and Method.* Rev. ed. Maryknoll: Orbis Books, 1995.

Ugolino di Monte Santa Maria. *The **Little Flowers** of St. Francis of Assisi.* Trans. and ed. W. Heywood. New York: Vintage Books, 1998.

APPENDIX

A Step-by-Step
Guide to the Prayer Practices

Under each chapter heading you will find instructions for doing the featured prayer practice either as an individual or in a group.

1 SOLITUDE AND SILENCE: THE JOURNEY BEGINS

Solitude and silence are the basis for most of the practices described in the book. Here are some general tips and guidelines to help you become comfortable with these two cornerstones of contemplation.

FOR AN INDIVIDUAL

- Begin the practice by noting your intention to spend more time in solitude and silence. All the practices in the book begin with such an act of intention: We make a positive statement to ourselves and to God that we desire a deeper awareness and experience of the divine.

- Begin to notice times when you are already in solitude and/or silence—when you take a walk, when you are in the car alone, when you are at home by yourself, when you go to the gym to work out.

- During these times, consciously bring to mind your intention to pray. Ask God to help you notice the presence of Jesus in your life. Address God with any specific questions or concerns you might have about your spiritual life.

- Listen for the reply from God. Don't be concerned if nothing happens. Continue to bring your mind back to God in the silence.

꩜ Over time, pay attention to your desires regarding your prayer life. Perhaps you find yourself wanting to pray more. Perhaps you find your life changing in various ways. If you find yourself desiring more silence and solitude, respond to these desires. Go on a retreat, take up some of the other practices in the book, spend more time alone with God.

FOR A GROUP

꩜ First the group makes a commitment to spend more time in silence together. This commitment could be made during an opening prayer time or as part of a structured activity.

꩜ The group chooses or the leader suggests how to create times of solitude and silence for the members. After such times, the group debriefs together. For example, group members might go for a fifteen-minute walk, spend some time praying silently in the sanctuary, or have time to do another silent prayer practice alone.

꩜ The group gathers to share experiences of solitude and silence. Everyone is invited to talk without trying to fix one another's problems or reinterpret others' personal experiences. The group leader needs to have enough experience with solitude to be able to offer constructive feedback if it seems necessary.

꩜ Group members pray for one another as a means of supporting their spiritual journey. They may pray for God to give them strength for moving into deeper solitude and silence.

2 *LECTIO DIVINA*: ENCOUNTERING SCRIPTURE THROUGH SACRED READING

Lectio divina, or "divine reading," is a powerful way to encounter God in scripture and offers a wonderful practice for either individuals or groups. The individual practice has four phases. The group practice can be adapted to fit the setting; here I describe a three-phase group practice.

INDIVIDUAL *LECTIO DIVINA*

✐ Phase 1, *Lectio* (reading/listening)

- Choose a passage of scripture. Although any passage will do, a psalm, a story about Jesus, or one of the poetic passages from a prophet works very well. For example, try Mark 1:14-20 or Isaiah 40:1-5.

- Read the passage to yourself twice. Don't be caught by the literal meaning of the scripture. Rather, listen for the word or phrase that catches your attention.

- Silently focus on that word or phrase. Repeat it a few times. Allow it to sift through your heart and mind.

✐ Phase 2, *Meditatio* (pondering)

- As you continue to focus on your word or phrase, pay attention to the thoughts and feelings it evokes.

- What images, what thoughts, what memories come to mind?

- Continue to ask God to speak to you through this word, and continue to listen for the reply.

✐ Phase 3, *Oratio* (responding)

- At some point you may find yourself wanting to reply to God. What desires has your prayer awakened in you?

- Maybe you have found an area of your life that needs some work.

- Maybe you find you are grateful for something and you wish to express that gratitude.

- Maybe you feel called to a new course of action in your life.

- Whatever you sense, do not rush the prayer. Continue to wait and listen as God forms your prayer and desire in your heart.

Speak your prayer of desire, longing, or action to God. Continue to listen in the silence.

ᕿ Phase 4, *Contemplatio* (resting)

- In this final phase of the prayer, the conversation with God draws to a close. Having heard a word from God and having expressed your response to that word, you now allow yourself to rest in the silence.

- Allow your mind to settle.

- When you feel that the prayer has come to an end, express your gratitude to God. This can be as simple as saying "Thank you" or "Amen."

LECTIO IN A GROUP

This process follows closely the individual process except that at the end of each phase, the group members are invited to speak the results of their prayer.

ᕿ Phase 1

- The group leader reads a Bible passage aloud twice.

- In the silence each person begins to listen for the word or phrase in the passage that speaks to him or her.

- After a period of silence, the group leader invites the group to share aloud their word or phrase. (People are to speak only their word, not commenting on its importance to them.)

ᗇ Phase 2

- The group leader reads the passage aloud again.

- This time, the group leader invites participants to wait for an image, thought, or phrase that arises in response to the passage.

- After another time of silence, the leader invites group members to share what they received in the silence.

ᗇ Phase 3

- The leader reads the passage a third time.

- The group members are invited to listen for how God is speaking to them through the passage.

- After a time of silence, the group is invited to share what they have heard in this phase of the prayer.

ᗇ Phase 4

- After everyone finishes sharing, the group could close the time of prayer with an expression of gratitude: a brief verbal prayer or a moment of silence.

In the group process, it is important that group members not comment on one another's observations but simply listen during the sharing period.

3 THE JESUS PRAYER: THERE IS POWER IN HIS NAME

FOR AN INDIVIDUAL

ᗇ Decide how long you wish to spend in prayer. At first you might try just fifteen minutes. You may want to spend more time as the prayer becomes familiar.

ᗇ The Jesus Prayer can be done anywhere—as you take a walk, in your office, on the bus, late at night in bed, in a church.

ᗇ Repeat, in your mind, "Jesus Christ, Son of God, have mercy on me."

- The repetition should be continuous; that is, the phrase is to be spoken again and again.

- Allow the words to flow into your entire being.

- When you have completed your time of prayer, express your thanks to God.

For a Group

- The leader sets or the group decides on the amount of time to pray.

- The group members may wander as space permits; members may choose a place to pray; or the group may decide on a location.

- Group members individually practice the prayer as described above.

- When the group gathers again, each member has an opportunity to share his or her experience. The purpose of this time is not to fix one another's problems or determine who prayed "correctly."

- The group leader needs to be prepared to give encouragement and support to group members who feel they "don't get it."

- Group members can encourage one another to try the prayer on their own.

4 Apophatic Prayer: Be Still and Know

Apophatic prayer is the simplest prayer and perhaps the most difficult. It is helpful to do this prayer more than once, as the experience of the prayer on any given occasion can be good or bad, and either is perfectly correct.

For an Individual

- Decide on a length of time for the prayer, usually twenty to forty-five minutes. A shorter time may be preferable for beginners.

- Pick a word to use as a point of focus during the prayer. It doesn't matter what word you choose as long as it reminds you of God's presence.

- Find a quiet place to sit. It is helpful to sit in a good upright posture, with your hands resting on your thighs. Generally this prayer is done with eyes closed. If that is uncomfortable, then allow your gaze to rest on the floor six to eight feet in front of you.

- Begin your prayer by silently saying your word once. Then just sit quietly. Unlike the practice of Jesus Prayer, the word is not to be repeated continuously.

- When you notice that you have become distracted by your thoughts, silently repeat the word to bring yourself back to the present.

- When your time of prayer has ended, express your gratitude to God.

FOR A GROUP

- Select a comfortable space for your prayer time. Arrange the seating so people are not facing one another. Decide how long the group will be in prayer.

- One person will begin and end the time of prayer. In addition, a small bell may be used to begin and end the time of prayer.

- The leader begins the time of prayer by saying, "Let us pray."

- Group members then do the practice as described above for the set period of time.

- The leader ends the time of prayer by reciting the Lord's Prayer.

- When the prayer is over, it is valuable to provide a time for group discussion. During this time, the most helpful comments from the leader simply assure people that they are not doing the prayer incorrectly and encourage them to go back to their word during the prayer.

5 THE EXAMEN: GOD IN DAY-TO-DAY LIFE

FOR AN INDIVIDUAL

☙ Choose a period of time to examine in prayer. This can be a day, a week, or a specific event.

☙ Allow your mind to wander through that period of time. Some questions you might ask yourself about that period include:

- What am I most/least grateful for during that time?
- When did I feel a sense of love, peace, joy, life (the gifts of the Spirit)?
- When did I feel exhausted, dead, drained, angry, mean?
- What specific events, thoughts, or experiences draw my attention?
- What aspects of that time repel me?
- What moments from that time speak to me of my deepest desires?
- What things feel out of place, uninteresting?

☙ Ask yourself, *When did I notice God during this time? What felt like a time of God's absence?*

☙ As some answers to these questions arise, notice what this tells you about the future. How is it that God is calling you into being? Toward what actions, activities, or attributes is God drawing you?

☙ Repeat this prayer at regular intervals in order to see how God is working in your life.

FOR A GROUP

A group may do the examen in two ways: (1) Each individual in the group does an examen and shares the results with the others; (2) the group applies the examen to an activity or time that group members experienced in common.

CR Method 1

- Each group member receives the instructions provided above for an individual and then takes a period of time, specified by the group or leader, to do the examen.

- When that time is up, the group members share their experiences. The group serves as a place for support, affirmation, and feedback for each individual.

CR Method 2

- The group that gathers to do the examen has participated in some common activity, such as a worship service, a planning process, an outing, or a mission activity.

- The group practices the examen on this common activity. Each member of the group is given some time to pray over the activity, using the individual steps above.

- Then the group shares the results of their prayer. This provides an opportunity to see the many ways God is working in the common activity. It also gives the group a chance to see things that are "not of God."

- The group can use these reflections to guide its future activities.

6 Creativity and the Divine: To Create Is to Pray

For an Individual

☙ Begin by noting your intention to notice God through your creative actions. Notice what activities you already do that involve creativity. Also notice any desires for creative activity that you do not currently do. These things could include but are certainly not limited to:

- Decorating your house or room
- Getting dressed
- Art in school or other settings
- Cooking
- Your ministry or other job
- Activities in which you and your friends participate
- Writing projects

☙ As you do these activities, bring to them an attitude of prayer. Ask God to help you seek Jesus during your time of creativity.

☙ Notice what happens during these prayer times.

☙ Give thanks to God.

For a Group

☙ The group leader selects a creative activity, usually some form of artwork.

☙ Make sure plenty of art supplies are available.

☙ Members of the group pray creatively for a set amount of time. They may leave the group meeting place or all work in the same area. The point is not to make a finished piece of art but rather to use the creative time as an opportunity to converse with God.

☙ When the time is over, the group gathers together and shares observations about the creative experience.

Combining Creativity with Other Prayers

For either an individual or a group, creative practice may be combined with other prayers. For example, you might spend time drawing after a *lectio* prayer or after the examen. Or get out art supplies after taking a walk in silence and see what happens. There are many possibilities. Combining creative prayer with another practice works particularly well in a retreat setting.

7 Journaling: Writing What God Shows Us

Basic Journaling. This practice can be done either by an individual or in a group setting. Simply take time to allow yourself to write about your thoughts, your desires, your questions in relation to God. Pray to God on paper. Watch as your relationship with Jesus deepens and grows over time. In the group setting, these observations and reflections can be shared as a means of support.

Conversation with God. This specific writing practice can be done alone or in a group setting.

- Express your desire to have a conversation with God.

- Draw a line down the center of a piece of paper.

- The left side is for your words; the right side is for God. You are the scribe for both of you.

- Begin the conversation with your side. Write down your thoughts, questions, concerns, or anything on your mind.

- Listen for any replies. Write down whatever seems appropriate on the right side of the page. As strange as this sounds, you may be surprised at the results of this prayer!

- In the group setting, share your conversation with others.

Wall of Prayer. This exercise can be considered a group journaling or creative prayer project.

- You will need a fairly large table and a long piece of butcher paper.

- Lay the paper out on the table. Place paints, markers, pens, and other art supplies all over the paper so that they are accessible to people standing around the table.

- Gather the group around the table and provide some beginning point for the prayer: a topic, a piece of scripture, or a question.

- People begin to write and draw their prayers in response to the starting point.

- After ten minutes or so, everyone moves to a different place on the paper and begins to work again.

- When the time for prayer is over, hang the paper on a wall so all can see the the group's prayers.

8 Body Prayer: The Body and the Spiritual Life

Breath Prayer. This prayer can be done by an individual or in a group setting.

- Designate a length of time to pray. This prayer can be done in almost any setting—while walking, sitting, or lying down.

- Note your intention to experience God through your body. Ask God to make you aware of the presence of the Spirit in your breath.

- Draw your attention to your breathing. Try to breathe from your diaphragm, letting your abdomen rise and fall easily. Don't force your breath or breathe too quickly.

- Whenever your thoughts wander, bring your attention back to your breath. Pay attention to the breath of life filling your body.

- When the time of prayer is over, notice your feelings and the state of your mind. Thank God for this experience.

- If in the group setting, members may share experiences.

Body Sculpture. This is a group prayer practice that can be described as a physical *lectio divina.*

- Find a room with an open area where group members can create the body sculptures. The leader selects a passage of scripture and then reads the passage aloud twice.

- The leader reads a single word from the passage. The word should be read twice.

- In the silence that follows, members of the group, as they feel called to do so, go to the open area and form a sculpture with their body in response to the word. They hold their postures.

- After it seems that all who wish to create a sculpture have done so, the leader again reads the word. This is the signal for all to return to their seats.

- Repeat this process for several different words in the original scripture passage.

- Afterward, take some time to share your experience of the prayer with one another. Combining this practice with a creative art activity works well.

9 WALKING TOWARD GOD: THE JOURNEY MADE VISIBLE

Slow Walk. This is another practice appropriate for both individual and group prayer.

- Set a length of time for the prayer—at least fifteen minutes. If you are doing the prayer in a group, designate a route for your walk. This can be a circle in a room or some other configuration outside.

- Begin with an intention to listen for God with your whole being as you move through space.

- Start walking slowly. With each step, slow your pace. Eventually try to take one step every fifteen to thirty seconds (this will feel very slow).

- Pay attention to your breath, your body, your heart and mind. Whenever you become distracted, focus on the sensation of your feet contacting the floor with each step.
- At the end of the prayer, give thanks to God.
- In the group setting, take some time to reflect together on the practice.

Labyrinth. These first instructions apply to both individuals and groups. Following are additional notes for a group practice.

- Find a labyrinth. There may be one at a church or retreat center in your community. Locating a labyrinth can be the biggest obstacle to doing this practice.
- There are three phases to the practice: the walk in, resting at the center, and the walk out.
- Walking into the labyrinth is a time for shedding anything that keeps you from communion with God. You may want to silently repeat a scripture as you journey. Or take the time to notice your thoughts and feelings and consider these questions:
  - What is it like to be on this journey?
  - Is there anything I need to let go of?
  - Is there something blocking me from experiencing God's love?
  - Am I in need of forgiveness?
  - Do I need to forgive?
- The center of the labyrinth is seen as the point of unity with God, the symbolic dwelling place of God. When you arrive at the center, simply rest in God. Remain there as long as you like. Converse with God in whatever way seems appropriate to you.
- The walk out of the labyrinth is the process of bringing God back out into the world with you. As you retrace your steps, continue your prayer and conversation with the divine.

- In what new way might Jesus accompany you into the world?

- What are your thoughts and feelings as you contemplate going back out into your life?

- Do you come with any new insights, experiences, or plans?

◌ When you finally leave the labyrinth, give thanks to God for your time there.

ADDITIONAL INSTRUCTIONS FOR A GROUP

◌ When entering the labyrinth be sure to allow space between individuals. Sometimes it is helpful to post a person at the entrance to signal each person when to proceed into the labyrinth.

◌ As you are walking, feel free to pass others you meet. Go at your own pace.

◌ Watch the other people as they walk. Notice that you are all journeying to God as the body of Christ.

◌ After walking the labyrinth, take some time to share feelings and observations about the prayer.

10 PRAYING IN NATURE: CONTEMPLATION AND CREATION

General Prayer with the Natural World. This prayer is similar in form to the general prayer of solitude and the general prayer of creativity. In this prayer, you simply begin to turn your attention to God when you find yourself in natural settings. In addition you can intentionally plan to spend time in nature to be with God. This prayer can be done alone or in a group.

◌ Make known to God your intention to listen for God's presence in nature.

◌ Then as you encounter a natural setting (while hiking or walking, gazing at a sunset or sunrise, seeing the moon at

night, catching a glimpse of an animal or beautiful flower),
bring your attention to God.

- ✑ Notice your thoughts and feelings.
- ✑ Notice the amazing beauty of creation.
- ✑ Become aware of the power of the natural world.
- ✑ Reflect upon the gift of your own life.
- ✑ Thank God for the time of prayer.
- ✑ In a group setting, take some time to share your experiences.

Combining Other Prayers with Natural Settings. As with creative
prayer, prayer in nature may be combined with other practices. Next
time you are in a beautiful place, pray the Jesus Prayer or do an examen. Take photographs for use in a worship service. Use the power
of God's presence in the natural world to help you with your other
prayer practices.

Deep Examination of Natural Item. This variation of the general prayer in nature works well in a group or retreat setting.

- ✑ Select a natural item for use in the prayer practice—a
  flower, a blade of grass, a rock, anything that catches your
  eye.
- ✑ Choose a specific length of time for the prayer. In the
  group setting, the leader may set the length. Anywhere
  from fifteen to thirty minutes is appropriate.
- ✑ Follow the instructions for the general prayer in nature
  listed above, focusing your prayer and your attention on
  the single item.
- ✑ Pray deeply into this one tiny piece of the created world.
- ✑ How is God speaking to you?
- ✑ At the end of your prayer time, you might want to journal about your experience or engage in creative prayer in
  response to what you have heard.
- ✑ In the group setting take some time to share reflections
  with one another.

11 PRAYER AND LIFE IN THE WORLD: THE RUBBER MEETS THE ROAD

Tithing. The aim of this prayer practice is to start giving away 10 percent of your gross income. You may give that money to a church, or you may give to any group doing the works of justice and peace. As Jesus says in the parable, "When you do it to the least of these, you are doing it to me" (Matt. 25:40, AP). It is important that you feel good about the church or other group to which you give the money; you need to believe that this group is working to manifest the kingdom of God. This feeling is different from feeling that the work of the group directly benefits you, which it may not.

Then the practice is simple: Give away your money—or at least try. Watch what happens as you attempt to do this. This practice will affect all aspects of your life, so it presents an opportunity to converse with God about many things: how you spend your time, how you spend your money, what is really important in your life.

The Impossible Project. This practice is most appropriate for a group that will be together for a while, such as a church group.

- Begin to pray together about the work that God is calling the group to do. The group might begin to do the examen on its mission.

- As time goes on, notice what longings and desires arise in the group. What is "tugging" on the group? What is God pushing the group to do and be in the world?

- After a while some specific suggestions may arise. Keep track of these. Don't discard any idea. Pay attention to which suggestions excite the group. Do the examen on a list of suggestions.

- Finally one or two ideas may grab the imagination of the entire group. These ideas probably will seem impossible— the projects too large, too expensive, too outlandish.

- Pick one of the projects and try to do it anyway.

ʒ Most importantly, as you proceed, continue to remain in prayer about the project. Because it is impossible, it is God's project, not yours; if you cease to pray, you will fail.

12 A PRAYING COMMUNITY: BRINGING IT ALL TOGETHER

As I mentioned in the chapter, there is no specific set of instructions for this practice. Listed below are attributes that I feel must be part of a praying community. For a description of these attributes, see the chapter:

ʒ Humility

ʒ Obedience to God

ʒ Empowerment of each community member by God

ʒ Prayer, both individual and group spiritual practices

ʒ Scripture

ʒ Relationships among community members characterized by the following attributes:

- Treating one another as you would treat Jesus
- Caring for one another
- Serving each other
- Being hospitable
- Honesty
- Trust

ʒ Community discipline that focuses on appropriate consequences for actions and honest appraisal of behavior

ʒ Leadership characterized by spiritual teaching

ʒ Stability—finding a way to consistently practice these attributes as a community over time

ʒ Some form of community work/service

ʒ Some form of community poverty

A Retreat Model

There are many ways to structure a prayer retreat, but all of them amount to the same thing: Take time to pray! I offer here a general outline of what a daylong prayer retreat might look like in a group setting. A few variations follow as well as notes about elements that could be added or deleted. The outline can be tailored to fit whatever time frame you have available (I have done prayer "retreats" that were one hour long!). If you are doing the retreat on your own, simply omit the group activities.

OUTLINE

Early morning: Worship prayerfully as a group.
Breakfast
Morning: Teach and do a prayer practice.
Lunch
Afternoon:

- Offer some free time.

- Teach and do another prayer practice, or repeat the same prayer practice you learned in the morning.

- Take some time for group reflection and sharing.

Supper
Evening: Prayerful worship.

POSSIBLE ADDITIONS

- Consider adding silence to all or part of the day.

- Add a talk on prayer or a scriptural meditation.

- Consider adding fasting as part of the retreat. Caution is in order regarding this decision. Special dietary needs or eating disorders may affect group members, so evaluate the situation before incorporating this element.

- Add a group reflection time in the morning.

- Offer individual spiritual direction as part of the retreat time.

- If you are in a beautiful setting, encourage people to take walks.

- If possible, add group work tasks as part of the retreat. The kitchen or dining hall offers good opportunities for simple tasks like meal preparation or just setting the table.

- Use a single passage of scripture as the theme for the whole retreat time.

- Create another type of theme to ground the retreat.

Above all when on retreat, have a wonderful, relaxing time with God!